An introduction to PEAF

Pragmatic Enterprise Architecture Framework

Kevin Lee Smith

Edited by Tom Graves

Published by

Pragmatic EA Ltd

25 Buttermere

Great Notley, Essex CM77 7UY

England

http://www.PragmaticEA.com

First published May 2011

ISBN 978-1-908424-00-6 (hardback)

ISBN 978-1-908424-01-3 (paperback)

ISBN 978-1-908424-02-0 (ebook)

Contents

"Computers are useless. They can only give you answers"

- Pablo Picasso.

Acknowledgements

The author would like to acknowledge the extensive help and advice provided by Tom Graves of Tetradian Consulting to get this book to market, particularly the **Application** sections which provide guidance on how to use the material.

Please note that, to preserve commercial and personal confidentiality, any stories and examples in this book will usually have been adapted, combined and in part fictionalised from experiences in a variety of contexts, and do not and are not intended to represent any specific individual or organisation.

Registered trademarks such as PEAF, Zachman, TOGAF, FEAF etc are acknowledged as the intellectual property of the respective owners.

The cover image was generated by **Wordle**™ (www.wordle.net) utilising all the words contained in this book.

FOREWORD

Failure

You may be wondering why I start a book with the word Failure.

Failure tends to be a dirty word. Failure tends to be hidden and, even if the subject is raised, is spoken about in hushed tones. Everyone wants to seem successful and therefore everyone tends to concentrate on success stories.

But this is a book about a Pragmatic approach to Enterprise Architecture. If you want to be pragmatic, the easiest thing to do is to learn from other people's mistakes. Advancement can come through success yes, but generally more advancement is born from failure, or rather understanding the reasons for that failure.

> *"Good decisions come from experience...*
> *Experience comes from bad decisions"*
>
> *- Anonymous.*

The important clarification here, however, is that you can either learn from making bad decisions or you can learn by observing others making bad decisions. The point is, you do not need to have made those bad decisions yourself, to have the experience to make good decisions.

Thus, PEAF is proudly born from failure: from observing (and participating in) numerous companies' attempts at Enterprise Architecture in varying guises, scales and approaches, and from understanding the reasons for those failures and creating products and processes to ensure as much as possible that those mistakes will not be repeated.

Every part of PEAF exists to plug a hole – holes that will either seriously derail attempts at an Enterprise Architecture initiative or will ultimately guarantee its failure.

This is not some ivory-tower purist approach to Enterprise Architecture. This is a super low-fat boiled-down set of products and processes required to be successful. Allowing people to invest 20% of the effort to reap 80% of the benefits.

In many respects Enterprise Architecture can be compared to gardening – or more accurately the products, processes and tools and techniques that allow a gardener to produce a pleasant garden or to grow fruit and vegetables.

A lot of people try to "sell" Enterprise Architecture with quick wins and low-hanging fruit. Whilst we will certainly not ignore such opportunities if they exist, to pursue only those quick wins is totally against the raison d'être of Enterprise Architecture.

Enterprise Architecture is concerned with creating the correct *environment* for the gardener and the garden to be effective and efficient. Creating the correct *environment* does not in itself create the garden, but as every gardener will know, that *environment* can have a massive positive or negative impact on the garden. This is exactly the same for Enterprise Architecture - we are creating the *environment* required for an organisation (participating in an enterprise) to grow, to flourish, to bloom and to bear fruit - not only for this year but for next year and for many years to come. Implementing changes to become more mature in how Enterprise Architecture is utilised does not in itself do this, but provides the *environment* for this to happen.

Many gardeners also know you can try to create the correct *environment* through trial and error (and sometimes for specific reasons it is beneficial to do this), but generally speaking the best gardeners lever and utilise the tips, tricks and knowledge of other gardeners as much as possible. In this respect, they are architects.

There is a lot information about Enterprise Architecture. Much of it is conflicting, inconsistent, inapplicable or unusable. This is why PEAF was created - to provide a small and concise set of real things to use rather than long winded ivory tower opinion and explanations – knowledge that will allow the garden and the gardener to flourish.

Kevin Lee Smith
The Pragmatic Gardener

2

INTRODUCTION

Introducing PEAF

Enterprise-architecture addresses the real complexities inherent in large organisations and enterprises. It's a complex discipline in its own right: no surprise, then, that there are so many frameworks and methods and taxonomies and so on to support it. Yet whilst the theory of enterprise-architecture may be well-served at present – particularly so for any of the IT-oriented domains – there are still significant gaps in support for enterprise-architecture practice.

PEAF – the Pragmatic Enterprise Architecture Framework – is one of the few items available that explicitly aims to fill that gap. As its name suggests, it takes a strict pragmatic approach to every aspect of enterprise-architecture: a rallying-cry of "everything you need, and nothing you don't". And with its focus on the bald realities of everyday business – such as how to build executive 'buy-in', or when and how and why to set up the processes for governance in enterprise-architecture – it provides a welcome sense of *practicality* and realism that is often missing from other frameworks.

This book presents a practical introduction to PEAF version 2: a brief yet immediately-usable summary of its core concepts and pragmatic products and processes.

Like every framework, PEAF has its limits: for example, by intent, it has no predefined reference-architectures, and it holds a firm focus on the earlier stages of setting up and running an enterprise-architecture capability within an organisation. But for anyone who's just starting out on the enterprise-architecture journey, it would certainly be well worthwhile exploring all of the practical help and advice that PEAF can provide.

Who should read this book?

The book is intended for enterprise architects, business-architects, IT-architects, process-designers and others who deal with the practical implications of whole-of-enterprise issues.

It should also be useful for strategists and service-managers, and for anyone else who works with other enterprise-wide themes such as supply-chains, value-webs, quality, security, knowledge-sharing, sustainability, business ethics and social responsibility, or health, safety and environment.

What's in this book?

The text is divided into three main sections:

- overview and core fundamentals
- documents, templates and other PEAF 'products' to get you started
- the three groups of processes in the PEAF architecture-cycle

As with PEAF itself, there's a strong emphasis on practicality – on how to *use* each of the items in real-world practice. (For best value, though, it's best to read this book in parallel with the formal PEAF specification, which can be accessed for free from Pragmatic EA's website at www.pragmaticea.com.) Each chapter ends with a brief 'Applications' section, providing suggestions on how to apply the material in your own business context. And the book ends with a 'Resources' section, pointing to sources for further information on PEAF and other related frameworks and techniques.

But what *is* the Pragmatic Enterprise Architecture Framework? Let's start with a brief overview.

Context

Architecture is all about structure. That not only means the structure of the thing of interest, but also understanding the structure of the bigger picture – how the thing of interest fits into and relates to a wider picture.

This definition of architecture applies to everything, including EA itself. If we want to understand more about EA we have to look at the bigger picture to see how EA and other things fit into that bigger picture.

The Enterprise

Let us first consider and understand the differences and relationships between *The Enterprise*, *The Market*, *The Organisation* and the fundamental parts of the organisation as shown in the diagram below.

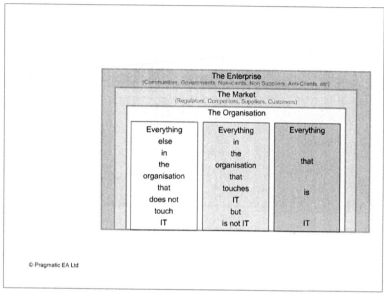

The Enterprise, The Market and The Organisation

We can see that *The Organisation* (split into three parts to be better able to represent the mapping of various frameworks) operates in the context of *The Market* which operates in the context of *The Enterprise*. We will map various popular frameworks onto this basic representation.

The Zachman Framework

We can now use this base diagram and overlay the Zachman framework (or ontology) to see how it relates to this structure.

The Enterprise, The Market and The Organisation+ Abstraction

The Zachman framework (or at least the rows) allow us to see the different levels within *The Enterprise, The Market* and *The Organisation.*

Some levels are wholly contained within *The Organisation* such as Planning, Change Projects and Running the organisation, while others such as the Contextual (or Strategy) level involves considering the wider market and the much wider Enterprise, and spans *The Enterprise, The Market* and *The Organisation.*

The Open Group Architecture Framework (TOGAF)

Using this as a base we can now overlay an Enterprise IT Architecture Framework (EITA) such as TOGAF to see how that relates to this wider context.

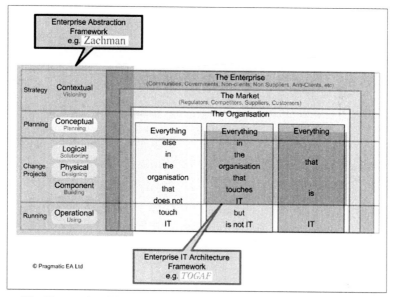

The Enterprise, The Market and The Organisation + Abstraction + EITA

We can see how an EITA framework such as TOGAF covers all the Logical, Physical and Component Layers and also some part of the Conceptual or Planning layer. It does not concern itself with anything in *The Organisation* that does not touch IT and therefore only covers a small part of the Conceptual or Planning layer. It largely ignores *The Market* and totally ignores *The Enterprise*.

The Pragmatic EA Framework (PEAF)

If we now add an EA Framework such as PEAF, we can begin to see where EA relates to the base-diagram and to the other frameworks we have considered thus far.

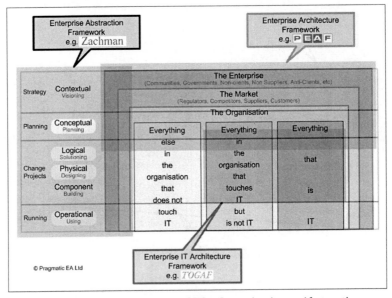

The Enterprise, The Market and The Organisation + Abstraction + EITA + EA

The important things to consider are:

1. EA scope is larger than *The Organisation*.

2. EA scope is larger than *The Market* which *The Organisation* operates within.

3. EA considers the entire breadth of *The Organisation* and its context, of which IT is a part, but only a part.

4. EA is mostly concerned with Strategic planning and the governance of Change projects.

The IT Infrastructure Library (ITIL)

For completeness we also add an IT Service Management Framework (ITSM) e.g. ITIL (IT Infrastructure Library) to see how this relates to the overall picture.

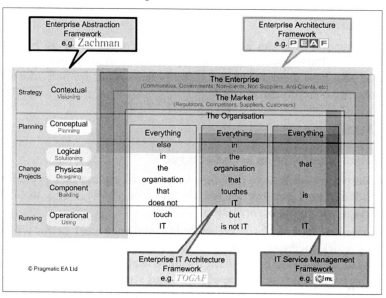

The Enterprise, The Market and The Organisation + Abstraction + EITA + EA + ESMF

We can see that ITIL is all about the Management of running IT Services although it does try to relate those operating services up to the level of change projects and strategy.

Like most things, these frameworks are not in competition but actually work in unison and complement each other.

Understanding where they sit and how they relate to each other (the Architecture of Frameworks) will help the reader in their understanding and application of them.

OVERVIEW

Summary

This section provides a quick overview of what PEAF is, how it relates to the overall business-discipline of enterprise-architecture, and also how it relates to and complements other frameworks for enterprise-architecture.

Details

What is enterprise architecture?

Enterprise architecture (EA) is a business discipline that provides guidance and governance for all types of strategic and tactical change within the organisation.

In essence, its most basic principle is that things work better when they work together, on purpose, especially over the longer term. Part of its role is to ensure that the organisation makes the best use of its various resources, capabilities and structures, and adapts to the organisation's changing needs over time. EA has a particular focus on optimising efficiency, effectiveness, agility and durability across the enterprise as a whole.

In the past it's often been associated primarily or even exclusively with IT – in fact some EA frameworks and models mention almost nothing else. In recent years, though, there has been a growing awareness that whilst IT is undoubtedly complex and important, it only makes sense within the context of the whole, and hence that 'enterprise architecture' must literally mean 'the architecture of the enterprise' in the broadest sense. PEAF was one of the first architecture-frameworks to incorporate this broader scope within its own structure.

What is PEAF?

The Pragmatic Enterprise Architecture Framework (or PEAF, for short) is a defined set of processes and related 'products' or documents to support decision-making, particularly in business change and investments for change.

PEAF is described as "a vendor and consultancy independent, technology neutral Enterprise Architecture Framework which allows organisations to kickstart or re-start an EA initiative". Its core is a comprehensive set of products and processes for EA – "everything required to hit the ground running".

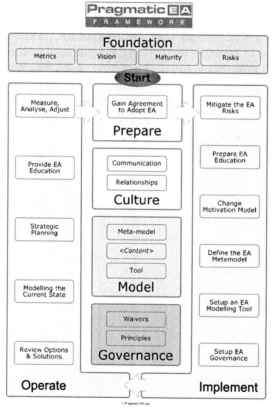

The Pragmatic EA Framework

PEAF is licensed in two forms: a non-commercial licence, which is free for individuals, end-user organisations, government bodies and academic institutions; and a full commercial licence, for consultancies, tool-vendors and training-providers. (The ethos behind the two types of licence is that EA should be free for those that want to use it to improve their own organisations, but those who aim to make money from the framework itself should contribute financially to enable its improvement and expansion.) Over the past two years, well over a thousand organisations – from small teams to large multinationals – have licensed PEAF for use in their own EA efforts.

One licensee summarised his experience as follows: "PEAF takes the confusion out of EA. Its simplicity of design allows a person to easily learn, understand and implement EA, without a heavy background in business or IT. PEAF is a godsend in comparison to other much more convoluted and confusing EA frameworks."

What's different about PEAF?

Enterprise-architecture frameworks tend either to be 'minimalist', providing too little to be useful in practice; or 'monolithic', trying to cover every possible eventuality, and becoming too complex and unwieldy to be usable. PEAF aims to bridge this gap by 'cutting EA to the bone', providing everything that you need and nothing that you don't.

In essence, the Zachman framework is an ontology or taxonomy, a way to classify architectural entities: until recently it had no associated methods or processes at all. The Open Group Architectural Framework [TOGAF] does provide a very detailed set of methods, but at present its design is strongly focussed on IT: its view and usage of what it calls 'business architecture' has been summarised as "anything not-IT that might affect IT", and does not really describe the strategic drivers of the business from a *business* perspective. The [US] Federal Enterprise Architecture Framework (FEAF) – in effect mandated by law for US government organisations – focuses primarily on how the architecture is documented, with much less apparent emphasis on how that documentation is to be used in practice. And whilst the Zachman framework could be described as 'minimalist', TOGAF and FEAF are huge, each running to well over a thousand pages once all of their supplementary material is included. For most real organisations, that kind of complexity can easily seem impractical overkill.

By contrast, PEAF places its emphasis on the one practical issue that causes the most problems for EA efforts: how to get started and keep going, delivering real and verifiable results within the constraints and complex, challenging realities of any large organisation. In a sense, PEAF was born out of failure – out of identifying all the myriad of ways in which EA efforts fail in real business practice, and then devising ways to prevent these sources of failure from occurring.

In effect, PEAF asserts that architects already know how to do architecture: the architecture *itself* is not the core problem. Every industry has its own standard reference-models and technology standards, and methods for architectures in their various forms are already well-known and well-described. What causes most of the problems are the practical business-matters: establishing the right business-case, setting the scope, engaging with the right stakeholders, obtaining funding and business buy-in, linking with business-strategy, governance and so on. It's *those* concerns – those *practical* concerns – that PEAF aims to address. Hence the term *Pragmatic* EA, because it's only by fully addressing those pragmatic matters that an EA effort can achieve success.

Application

- What is your own view of the role of enterprise-architecture? Is it primarily about IT, or does it have a wider business scope?
- What are others' views about EA within your organisation? What role does EA play within your organisation?
- If an EA capability exists within your organisation, what frameworks and methods does it use? Why those particular frameworks and methods? And what is the general perception of the role and value of that unit to the business as a whole?

FUNDAMENTALS

Summary

This section explores some of the fundamental concepts and ideas that underpin PEAF. These include an emphasis on real-world pragmatism and on value and values; a scope that ultimately covers the whole enterprise rather than solely its information-technology; the centrality of people and culture; the need for consistent models and consistent governance; and an iterative approach to the overall development of the architecture.

Details

Pragmatism

PEAF has an almost unique emphasis on pragmatism. What could be achieved in theory is of far less importance than what can and must be achieved in practice, in the real-world business context. Pragmatism is essential to achieve and maintain business buy-in.

Products and processes

PEAF splits the architecture framework into two distinct groups: Products, and Processes.

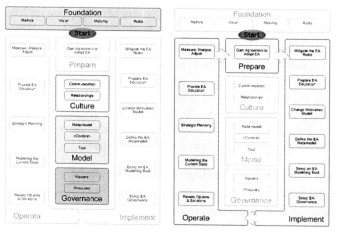

PEAF Products (left), Processes (right)

The Products group contains all the products needed to begin, document and guide an EA initiative:

- The *Foundation* section provides the products required for instigate and gain approval for an EA programme of work. Once these products are formulated, the board can quickly decide whether to pursue an EA initiative or not.
- The *Culture* section focusses on people and communication – the real key to EA. Without people and their understanding, everything else is superfluous.
- The main artefacts of EA are the *Models* that allow information to be gathered, viewed and analysed.
- The *Governance* products provide an environment to guide change as it happens throughout the organisation.

The Processes group in the framework contains all the processes required for an EA initiative, divided into three distinct phases:

- *Prepare* phase: Scoping and gaining approval for an EA initiative.
- *Implement* phase: Making the changes to prepare the organisation to operate EA.
- *Operate* phase: 'Doing' the architecture-work, guiding and assisting in organisational change.

(The relationships between Products and Processes are described in the detail-sections later in this book.)

An emphasis on value

A key driver throughout PEAF is the use of enterprise architecture to identify and deliver *demonstrable* business value.

Note that architecturally-relevant value may often exist in other than monetary terms. For example, an organisation's reputation and its internal and external relationships can have distinct value in their own right, as well as in terms of their indirect impact on monetary returns or costs. PEAF provides means to distinguish between the different forms of value, and also how they act upon each other to create the respective 'bottom-line'.

Monitoring and managing 'Enterprise Debt'

A central theme in PEAF is the concept of 'Enterprise Debt' – the effective costs and risks accumulated as a result of decisions in the past or present and carried forward into the future. One of the most important tasks of architecture is to identify, monitor and assist in managing the accumulated Enterprise Debt.

Enterprise Debt can arise from many sources, such as short-termism in business-decisions, or perhaps imposed by technical constraints. (Some technical constraints may be unavoidable, such as the historical constraints on data-storage space that led to the huge costs of 'Y2K'. And some Enterprise Debt arises more from the passage of time than anything else: legacy systems that can no longer be maintained, for example, or changes in law or regulation or technology that can change previous good design-decisions into liabilities.)

Once Enterprise Debt is incurred, it tends to accumulate a kind of 'interest', increasing the risk steadily further as time goes by. So business, technical and other decisions will need to be revisited, and strategies and tactics developed to mitigate the respective risk: hence a need for regular architecture-review, combined with appropriate governance to ensure that this takes place.

One of the key tasks of architecture in this is to help maintain an awareness of the whole, such that Enterprise Debt can most often be reduced via small adjustments to the role or scope of existing change-projects. The aim is always to avoid any need for specific 'fire-fighting' projects to address Enterprise Debt that has 'gone critical', such as occurred with Y2K.

As above, the value-types in the effective debt may not necessarily be in direct monetary form: for example, business decisions that damage reputation represent a form of 'debt' that can destroy the entire business in the longer term. Another aspect of the 'Y2K' example is that, over time, the skills to maintain and update the old legacy-code had become so rare that it was not a problem that money could solve: the scale of the problems was such that there were simply not enough people with the requisite skills to do the work, regardless of how much they could be paid.

In PEAF, Enterprise Debt is described in two forms.

- Enterprise Debt Value (EDV) – a 'point in time' measure of the amount of debt that has been built up in the entire enterprise.
- Enterprise Debt Ratio (EDR) – an indicator for the current project portfolio indicating the 'direction' or health of the current project portfolio in terms of Enterprise Debt, and in terms of how much of the work required is strategic, tactical or remedial.

When budgets and timescales are constrained (the bad times), the EDR of the enterprises' project portfolio is likely to trend towards increasing overall EDV, with projects concentrating more on the here and now, and hence creating more debt. In these periods, architecture should aim to keep the increase in accumulated-debt to the minimum practicable.

When budgets and timescales are more relaxed and forthcoming (the good times) the EDR of the enterprise's project portfolio should trend towards decreasing overall EDV. In these periods, architecture should take a pro-active role in identifying and 'paying off' the accumulated-debt.

More than just IT

In PEAF, the enterprise-architecture must be able to address *any* appropriate aspect of the enterprise – and not solely its IT, as is still the case in some other 'enterprise'-architecture frameworks.

PEAF layered view of architectures

This is illustrated in part by the placing of Business Architecture within PEAF's architecture-layers. 'Business Architecture' relates to the structure of business-processes and the like that are carried out by people; 'Technology Architecture' describes structures and the like to support those parts of the business-processes that are carried out by machines or other forms of automation, whether IT-based or not. The 'Enterprise Architecture' here relates to the strategic layer of the enterprise, whilst 'Solution Architecture' is about guidance and governance of projects and solution-designs to bridge between strategy and execution, and to create an appropriate balance between people, process and technology. As indicated by the 'jigsaw-puzzle', all of these 'architectures' must mesh together into a unified whole.

Culture

PEAF is almost unique in its emphasis on people – not technology – as the real core of the architecture: in fact it identifies enterprise-culture as a Critical Success Factor for enterprise-architecture. To put it at its simplest, an EA effort will succeed *only* if appropriate attention is paid to the 'people'-side of the architecture – and in particular, to all the communications, relationships, roles and responsibilities that underpin the architecture, and that come into contact with changing it in planning and execution.

One of the key points here is that, overall, enterprise-architecture is the responsibility of *everyone* – not solely the responsibility of people with 'architect' in their job-title. PEAF aims to support an organisational culture in which every person is committed to play their part in ensuring that "things work better when they work together", despite the difficulties of often-accelerating change.

Models

Whilst people are the key to enterprise-architecture success, the models and other artefacts form the backbone of any EA initiative. Over time, the set of models and related documents become a core part of the organisation's repository of information about the nature and structure of itself, and its objectives, goals, targets and strategies. This repository helps people to make better decisions and better judgements about changes to organisational structures, resources, processes and the like, whether those changes are self-chosen by the organisation or imposed from outside.

Although models do act as records of decisions and designs, it's crucially important that they become 'living documents' that are used and, as appropriate, updated by everyone involved – and not locked away in some 'ivory tower' or inaccessible system that only the specialists can see. In line with its focus on culture, PEAF insists that appropriate maintenance of models must ultimately be the responsibility of everyone.

Governance

Once again, governance in PEAF is viewed as the responsibility of everyone – not solely the responsibility of architects or project-managers. The focus is always on outcomes, not process: it's not about 'following rules' for the sake of it, but about getting things right in a pragmatic way. Governance is a key part of quality-control and risk-management, hence keeping to agreed principles, policies and standards should enhance quality and reduce risk, and also help to minimise and manage Enterprise Debt. If for any reason the principles and the like cannot be followed, proper governance ensures that the impacts, risks and other Enterprise Debt implications of not doing so are costed, understood, accepted and managed.

A key point regarding governance is that it should not be viewed as a policing environment where things are rejected and accepted or that penalties are incurred for breaking the rules. Instead, the approach must be culture based, with all stakeholders within the organisation (such as business, IS, project-managers and others) understanding the reasons *why* those principles, policies and standards exist, and how they contribute to move the organisation from where it is to where it wants to be.

Iterative process

Enterprise-architecture is not a project, a once-off 'fit and forget'; instead, it needs to be viewed as an ongoing strategic capability that, like quality-management, pervades through everything in the enterprise, and is the responsibility of everyone.

However, capability develops in line with maturity, which in turn grows through a cyclical, iterative process of planning, practice and review. To help in this, the PEAF processes are structured as a cycle, from Prepare to Implement to Operate, and back through review to Prepare for the next iteration. PEAF also provides an explicit maturity-model to guide reviews and to select capabilities to be developed further during the next cycle, to help in keeping everything on track towards the enterprise-vision.

Application

Compare the descriptions above to other enterprise-architecture frameworks that you know or use. In what ways do they differ in their fundamentals:

- What emphasis do they place on practicality rather than 'purity'? On realism and *usefulness* than idealised 'perfection'?
- What products and processes do they provide, to guide the practice of architecture?

- In what ways do they describe value? If value is described at all, is it described solely in monetary terms, or does it explore the deeper values from which monetary-value will ultimately arise?

- Does it provide any means to identify, monitor or manage Enterprise Debt? And does it provide any clear *business* reason – such as Enterprise Debt – to explain the purpose and value of enterprise-architecture?

- Does the scope describe anything much beyond IT? Does it place IT as the sole centre of its architecture-'world'? If it does describe a 'business architecture', in what ways does it distinguish between the strategic layer – 'the business of the business' – and the operational layer – what people do in 'the business', as 'business-processes'?

- What emphasis – if any – do they place on culture, or 'people-stuff' in general?

- What structures do they provide to support modelling?

- In what ways do they describe the practical processes of governance?

- And is the overall method iterative – a continuous cycle of improvement – or a once-off 'fit-and-forget' that's too easily forgotten?

- What do you learn from this comparison? What effects would each of these differences have on the way you practice enterprise-architecture in your organisation?

PRODUCTS: VISION

Summary

Before the main work can start, there needs to be clarity on the role of architecture itself. This part of the PEAF foundation should identify and document goals, strategies, tactics and objectives for EA, and where the discipline best fits within the organisation.

Details

This Foundation product summarises the strategies, tactics and objectives of adopting Enterprise Architecture, and the strategic goals of the enterprise that they flow from and help to achieve.

The purpose of the Vision product in PEAF is to ensure that the enterprise-architecture effort is linked back to the overall aims of the enterprise.

Once a clear vision of the work is in place that the stakeholders can understand, agree on and believe in, the architecture initiative will become meaningful and relevant throughout the enterprise.

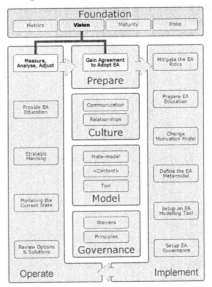

Processes using Vision

The Vision product is used mainly in the 'Gain Agreement To Adopt EA' tasks in the *Prepare* phase, and also for review in the 'Measure, Analyse, Adjust' tasks at the end of the *Operate* phase.

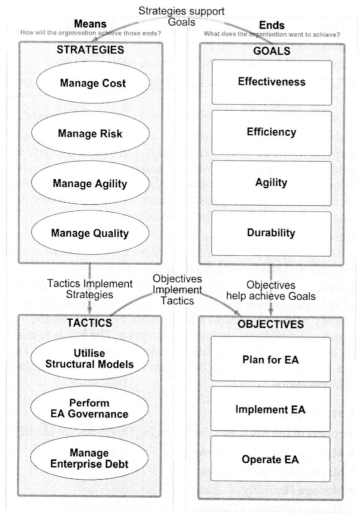

Overall rationale for enterprise-architecture

The 'rationale' diagram in PEAF summarises the key relationships between the generic enterprise aims or 'goals', the strategies to achieve them, and the architecture objectives and tactics needed to implement those strategies.

EA goals

The rationale to adopt enterprise-architecture and its products, processes, culture and tools arises from the need to satisfy four key aims or goals that apply to every enterprise:

- *Effectiveness*: 'do the right things', keep on track to enterprise purpose.
- *Efficiency*: 'do things right', do more, faster, with less.
- *Agility*: 'adapt quickly to the needs of the context', change faster with less.
- *Durability*: 'be effective, efficient and agile into the future'.

Durability is actually a component of the other three goals: an enterprise needs to be effective today, and efficient today, but it would be unwise to unknowingly compromise how effective or efficient it is likely to be tomorrow. Unless this time-component is built into the enterprise goals, the enterprise will be solely driven by the needs of now above the needs of tomorrow.

EA itself does not define any of these enterprise goals (or 'Ends'), but it does help to provide 'Means' by which they can be achieved effectively and efficiently both for today and into the future.

All of these goals are closely interlinked, and an over-focus on one goal can compromise the others. For example, aiming to increase efficiency without regard to effectiveness, agility or durability can have severe consequences for the enterprise. The key is to manage each of these competing goals, in balance and in parallel, and to make sound, informed decisions having considered the impact and implications.

EA strategies

In support of the EA goals, the following Strategies are identified

- Manage *Cost* of change etc
- Manage *Risk* of change etc
- Manage *Flexibility* of change etc
- Manage *Quality* of change etc

(Flexibility here includes adaptability and agility – the ability to adapt quickly to varying enterprise needs and pressures.)

In each case the aim is to *manage* the respective item, not always to reduce it: in some cases, and especially in the short-term, it may be necessary to increase costs or risks, or reduce flexibility or quality.

The goals are inherently related. If too much emphasis is placed on one, the system begins to break down and a downward spiral of negative feedback can begin. The key is to manage each of these competing strategies and to make sound informed decisions, having considered the impact and implications.

EA tactics

To support the EA strategies, PEAF identifies the following tactics:

- *Utilise Structural Models* – aid Strategic Planning via a flexible modelling-tool or toolset, extensible metamodel and processes for managing the models
- *Perform EA Governance* – manage alignment to the Strategic Plan via a set of principles, governance structure and processes for performing governance
- *Manage Enterprise Debt* – manage intangible debt by recording Enterprise Debt as it is created, and managing that Enterprise Debt as change happens during the year and during annual business planning.

The PEAF Vision product describes each of these tactical concerns in detail. In applying PEAF, the organisation will need to identify how to enact each of these tactics within its own context: the PEAF processes explain how to do this in real-world practice.

EA objectives

PEAF identifies the following objectives to support the EA tactics:

- 1: *Prepare for EA* – Setting out the business case for starting an EA initiative and gaining the required remit, budget and resources.
- 2: *Implement EA* – Making the necessary changes and adjustments to the enterprise identified in the Prepare phase, in preparation for it to be able to utilise Enterprise Architecture.
- 3: *Operate EA* – Utilising the products and processes set up in the Implementation phase to execute on the Strategies and Tactics and attain the goals of increased efficiency etc.

The PEAF processes form an iterative cycle to support each of these objectives. Each iteration of preparation, implementation and operation of EA builds on previous iterations; the increase in maturity over time leads to increased Effectiveness, Efficiency, Agility, and Durability.

EA role and purpose within the organisation

PEAF summarises the overall purpose of EA as follows:

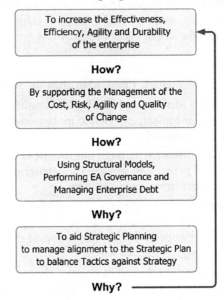

PEAF: the purpose of enterprise-architecture

Within the organisational jigsaw of processes, levels, disciplines, inputs, outputs and outcomes, the PEAF framework places enterprise-architecture primarily at the strategic level. The Vision product summarises this as follows, from strategy to execution:

Planning:

- *Contextual* layer – the board or other core governance body models the overall enterprise strategy, on behalf of shareholders and other stakeholders.
- *Conceptual* level – enterprise-architects create structural models and define a portfolio of principles and standards to guide solution-designs.

Change-projects:

- *Logical* layer – business-architects and solution-architects define high-level processes and abstract system-designs.
- *Physical* layer – business-analysts and technical architects define detailed business-processes and concrete system-designs.

- *Component* layer – business-analysts define procedures and work-instructions, and developers create applications and implemented systems.

Operations:

- *Operational* layer – end-users use the new or amended processes and systems to create value for the enterprise.

In essence, enterprise-architecture needs to become part of the culture that pervades an organisation. Importantly, though, the role of the enterprise-architecture unit needs to be understood as a *decision-support* function, not decision-making: the EA processes, models and other deliverables exist only to assist other people in the enterprise to make better strategic, tactical and operational decisions.

Enterprise-architecture is also not expensive: given the risks and costs of Enterprise Debt, *not* having good EA is likely to be *much* more expensive, especially in the longer term.

Implementation and operation of EA does make subtle changes to the organisation's existing structures, bodies and groups. The PEAF Vision product indicates that most of these differences would occur in the 'Business Change' parts of an organisation: in particular, the creation of a Strategic Investment Board, linked with an Enterprise Architecture Review Board, to support project-management and project teams in their decision-making.

Enterprise-architecture also introduces an EA Model to support and allow these changes to operate. The Vision product also includes a set of diagrams that detail the organisational 'touch-points' for the EA repository and its models and metamodels.

Application

- The term 'vision' seems to have many different meanings, especially in business, from 'desired outcome' to 'future state' to a description of the company's market-position or even an unchanging 'guiding star'. What meanings does it have within your organisation? What meanings does it have within your enterprise-architecture? What difficulties arise from the conflicts between all these different meanings?
- The PEAF Vision product provides a pragmatic 'starter-set' of definitions and directions for EA goals, strategies, tactics and objectives. Although these may well differ from those of EA in your own organisation, what do you see when you use the

PEAF set as a view into the organisation? What changes in the way you work, and the aims of your work, does this review suggest?

- What challenges do you face when setting out to embed an enterprise-architecture capability within the organisation? What vision do you need for EA, in order to engage others in this? How does that vision explain the *value* of enterprise-architecture to the organisation as a whole?

PRODUCTS: RISKS

Summary

Every project and capability will have a wide variety of associated risks and opportunities, with often-vocal objections to apparent risks. This section of the PEAF foundation describes how to identify, document and address the business risks for EA itself.

Details

The Risks product details common risks associated with bringing enterprise-architecture to an organisation. Most of these risks deal with people's misconceptions about the role and nature of EA.

Each defined risk documents the impact and general mitigation strategies to deal with that risk. A placeholder is left for specific mitigation strategies for each individual organization.

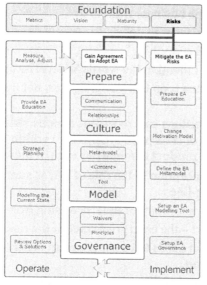

Processes using Risks

The Risks product is used mainly in the 'Gain Agreement To Adopt EA' tasks in the *Prepare* phase, and in the 'Mitigate the EA Risks' tasks in the early stages of the *Implement* phase.

Dealing with risks and objections

The Risks product presents a set of commonly-voiced objections to enterprise-architecture, the risks presented by each of these, and strategies and tactics to mitigate the risk. The objections listed in the Risks product are as follows:

- "It's just another silver bullet"
- "Nothing to do with me, mate!"
- "How much!?!"
- "Are we there yet?"
- "I have important firefighting to do..."
- "We don't live in a perfect world"
- "Oh what pretty pictures"
- "I can't afford a modelling tool!"
- "I don't want another maintenance nightmare"
- "How many paperclips do we have and who is using each one"
- "It's something consultants invented to get more money"
- "You can't define the future"
- "Don't tell the business what to do"
- "Don't tell IT what to do"
- "Let's model everything"
- "Shhh! Don't mention the words 'enterprise architecture'"
- "But my bonus is on this year's figures, not those in 2-5 years time"

All of these objections can represent serious risks to a successful roll-out and use of enterprise-architecture within the organisation. The PEAF Risks product summarises each of these as follows:

- *Risk* – misconception of the role of EA, as summarised by the objection tag-line
- *Description* – summary of the risk arising from the objection
- *Failure-impact* – the enterprise result if the risk eventuates
- *Reality* – what needs to be explained in order to overcome the misconception
- *Likelihood* – probability of the risk eventuating (low, medium, high)
- *Impact* – impact on the organisation if the risk does eventuate (low, medium, high)

- *Mitigation* – recommended strategies and tactics to mitigate the risk

For example:

- *Risk*: "It's just another silver bullet"
- *Description*: EA is perceived as a perfect fix for all of an organisations problems, with little or no work or cost
- *Failure-impact*: Other associated and related activities are overlooked and stagnate while the Nirvana that EA is supposed to provide, but will not, is created.
- *Reality*: EA is one tool in toolbox that an enterprise uses to run efficiently. It is linked to and cooperates with other processes in the enterprise.
- *Likelihood*: medium
- *Impact*: high
- *Mitigation*: Communication

Probably the most important part of risk-mitigation for enterprise-architecture is developing and actioning a clear communication strategy. The Communications section of PEAF's Culture product includes a full set of slidedecks to aid in this; these should be used in the 'Prepare EA Education' tasks in the *Implement* processes and the 'Provide EA Education' tasks in the *Operate* processes.

Application

- What objections do you hear about enterprise-architecture?
- What risks does each of these objections represent, both the EA and to the goals of the enterprise as a whole? What potential impacts does each of these risks have on your organisation's Enterprise Debt?
- What do you need to do to resolve each of those objections, and to mitigate each of those risks?
- By what means, and via what metrics, would you monitor the actual and potential impacts of each of those risks? How would you know when each of those risks has been reduced, and by how much they have been reduced?
- What part does an explicit Communication Strategy play in your EA risk-management? How do you action that strategy? And how do you monitor how well that strategy works?

PRODUCTS: MATURITY

Summary

An organisation's choices are constrained by the level of maturity that applies in each of its capabilities at that time. PEAF provides a straightforward maturity-model to identify the respective levels of maturity for an organisation's EA, and to guide choices for action to enhance that maturity.

Details

This Foundation product details a Maturity Model that describes maturity levels for each part and sub-part of the Framework. One dimension defines a set of levels, from 1 to 5. The other dimension consists of domains that align with the structure of the PEAF framework: Culture, Model, Governance, and the processes in the Operate phase. At the intersection of each, the maturity model defines the benefit of attaining that level, and the tasks and costs involved in moving to the next level.

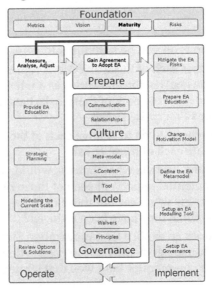

Processes using Maturity

The Maturity product is used mainly in the 'Gain Agreement To Adopt EA' tasks in the *Prepare* phase, and also for review in the 'Measure, Analyse, Adjust' tasks at the end of the *Operate* phase.

Maturity levels

The levels of the Maturity Model can be summarised as follows:

- *Level 1*: 'Nowhere' – the worst place to be.
- *Level 2*: 'Somewhere' – a step in the right direction.
- *Level 3*: 'Everywhere' – a reasonable target.
- *Level 4*: 'Cultural' – a 'stretch-target' for most organisations.
- *Level 5*: 'Optimised' – a possibly-unobtainable Nirvana

The model also describes what and how products and processes are in use at each level, and what the level represents in practice. For example, for Level 2, 'Somewhere':

- *Use of EA*: Products and Processes do exist but are not widely used or are used incorrectly.
- *Implications*: Promotion to this level indicates a step in the right direction even if that step is not very large or the benefits are not large.

These levels are based loosely on the CMMi model, but have been extended to include products as well as process maturity, and are aligned to pragmatic objectives.

Maturity categories

The categories used for maturity classification mirror the structure of PEAF:

- *Culture*: Communications, Relationships – nothing happens without communicating with people or without the right motivation
- *Model*: Metamodel, Model-content, Tools – the main product/resource of enterprise-architecture
- *Governance*: Principles, Waivers – definitions of guiding principles and recording deviation from them
- *Operate*: Culture: EA Education; Model: Strategic Planning, Current State; Governance: Options & Solutions – the key operational processes

The remainder of the Maturity Model is based on the intersections between these levels and categories.

Maturity evidence

This section of the Maturity Model details the evidence that would serve to indicate which Level an enterprise has attained in each of the Categories. For example, for the 'Model' section of Level 2, 'Somewhere':

- *Metamodel*: a baseline "current" Metamodel exists; the baseline Metamodel allows the capture of the most important entities and relationships for the organization.
- *Model-content*: the model has enterprise-wide scope and shows a clear line of sight between the Business and IS.
- *Tools*: a proper EA modelling toolset is in use; use of the toolset is limited to EA team and specific areas of IS; interfaces to sources of information are largely manual and ad-hoc

These evidential statements are not hard and fast rules, but are used to provide a basis for organisations to get a feel for their current level of EA Maturity and to help guide them to decide what level of maturity they wish to attain and in what timescales.

Maturity transitions

This section details the transitions from one level to the next.

For each of the transitions, a set of benefits is listed, indicating the anticipated outcomes of moving from one level to the next.

Each transition also lists a set of tasks to be undertaken to allow the transition to occur. The number in brackets after each task is a high level estimate of the number of days of effort that would be required to complete that task.

For example, for the transition from Level 2 to Level 3 for the 'Model: Metamodel' section:

- *Benefits*: allows more detailed information to be gathered for each "current" entity which provides more information to make better decisions; allows relationships to strategic vision, drivers and objectives to be understood.
- *Tasks*: expand baseline 'current' Metamodel (10 days); define/Agree baseline 'strategy' Metamodel (5 days)

Note that the time-estimates shown in this section are in person-days, not elapsed-time. Elapsed time could be less (if more people are involved) or more (if other work is required). The estimates are provided to give a feel for the amount of effort that would be required.

Application

- What maturity-models do you already use in your organisation, for EA and other capabilities? By what means do you monitor and measure maturity for each of the capabilities across the enterprise?
- What guidance – if any – does each maturity-model provide as to how to move from one maturity-level to the next?
- What is the maturity-level of your own organisation's enterprise-architecture, and its EA capability? What do you need to do, to move it up to the next level?

PRODUCTS: METRICS

Summary

Metrics are essential to identify and track maturity-levels in the various parts of the organisation. This section of the foundation in PEAF describes typical metrics used to track the maturity of EA itself.

Details

This Foundation product details the metrics that monitor and measure how the enterprise-architecture effort is helping the organisation and delivering on its goals and objectives.

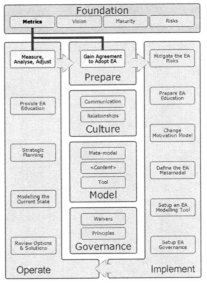

Processes using Metrics

The Metrics product is used mainly in the 'Gain Agreement To Adopt EA' tasks in the *Prepare* phase, and in reviews in the 'Measure, Analyse, Adjust' tasks at the end of the *Operate* phase.

These metrics are used in conjunction with the maturity-model described in the PEAF Maturity product.

Maturity-metrics for EA

The maturity-metrics are categorised by Process and task within Process, and Product or sub-Product used within that process or task. Note that metrics may be quantitative, qualitative or simple checkbox-type 'Yes/No' flags: the key concern in each case is that it provides a means to identify and monitor the respective aspect of EA maturity.

(See the 'Processes using...' and 'Products used by...' diagrams in each of the Products and Processes chapters: each link between Product and Process in a diagram also represents a category of EA metrics.)

For example, Metrics itself has metrics for its use in the tasks '*Prepare*: Gain Agreement to Adopt EA' and '*Operate*: Measure, Analyse, Adjust'.

Metrics in the *Prepare* phase tend to be simple Yes/No checklists. For example, for the Vision product in 'Gain Agreement to Adopt EA' has the following checklist-metrics:

- Does a defined EA Vision exist?
- Has the EA Vision been signed off?

Some numeric metrics do occur in the *Prepare* process, such as for Metrics itself, in the 'Gain Agreement to Adopt EA' task:

- Number of metrics that exist.
- Percentage of metrics that are being used to evaluate EA effectiveness

The metrics used in the *Implement* phase are a similar mix of checklist-type and numerics, such as for Communications in the 'Prepare EA Education' task:

- Has a set of EA implementation and operation training materials been obtained?
- Percentage of the board that have received EA training
- Percentage of the Executive Management that have received EA training

In the *Operate* phase, more of the metrics are numerics rather than checklist-type, as shown for the Governance Principles product in the 'Review Options & Solutions' task:

- Percentage of projects being reviewed against the principles
- Percentage of projects that have a Business Problem Definition document

- Number of Agreements to change Solution/Options
- Number of Solution/Options Escalated to SIB [Strategic Investment Board]
- Number of Solutions Escalated to SIB

As with the maturity-evidence criteria, the final set of EA metrics will vary somewhat from one organisation to another, according to needs and context. The aim of this PEAF product is to provide a 'starter set' that is known to work well for the initial needs for EA monitoring in most types of organisations.

Application

- What metrics do you use to monitor the impact of enterprise-architecture on managing change, and the effectiveness of change, within the organisation?
- What metrics do you use to monitor and manage the operation of enterprise-architecture itself?
- In what ways do each of these metrics link back to the core organisational goals? In what ways do they link back to the overall management of enterprise opportunities and Enterprise Debt?

PRODUCTS: CULTURE

Summary

Cultural issues and concerns – communication, relationships and responsibilities in particular – can make or break any enterprise-architecture effort. This section of the PEAF products helps to address this.

Details

The Culture section of PEAF addresses the 'people' aspects of enterprise-architecture.

This set of materials deals with communication about enterprise-architecture, and assesses relationships between people and the various groups that exist within an organisation. It also provides lists of the resources required to prepare, implement and operate enterprise-architecture. Job-descriptions and Terms of Reference are provided for key individuals and groups.

These products, when coupled with the preparation work in the *Implement* phase, and the provision of training and education in the *Operate* phase, are probably the most important of all the PEAF products.

This is also the hardest part of the work to get right and the easiest to overlook – key reasons why so many EA initiatives fail.

Communication

This part of the Culture products consists of a set of Powerpoint slidedecks to aid in explaining the role, function and scope of EA, and in training and educating people in how to work with and make the best use of EA and its models and other artefacts.

These slidedecks are used or referenced in the following tasks:

- *Prepare* phase: 'Gain Agreement to Adopt EA'
- *Implement* phase: 'Prepare EA Education'
- *Operate* phase: 'Provide EA Education'

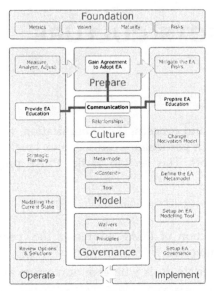

Processes using Communications

The current version of PEAF provides the following slidedecks in the Communication section of the Culture product:

- EA – Why I Don't Need It!
- EA – Frameworks
- EA – Enterprise Debt
- EA – EA Model vs CMDB
- EA – Traits of an Enterprise Architect
- Overview – Pragmatic EA Ltd
- Overview – PEAF
- PEAF – Products: Foundation
- PEAF – Products: Culture
- PEAF – Products: Model
- PEAF – Products: Governance
- PEAF – Processes: Prepare
- PEAF – Processes: Implement
- PEAF – Processes: Operate

Further slidedecks and other support-materials are available from the PEAF website and community.

Relationships

The Culture products also include a Relationships section. This is in two parts, the first of which explores the relationships between people and the various groups that exist within an organisation, from the perspective of enterprise-architecture. A framework cannot create or fix relationships within an organisation, but it can highlight the frames within which those relationships exist, and the fundamentals of those relationships. It also provides a frame through which to model those relationships, to understand the impacts they have and how they may need to be modified.

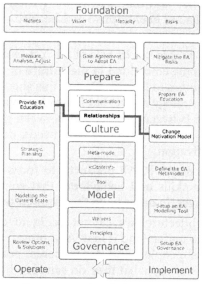

Processes using Relationships

The Relationships and responsibilities section within the Culture products is used in the 'Change Motivation Model' tasks within the *Implement* phase, and in the 'Provide EA Education' tasks in the *Operate* phase.

The main function of enterprise-architecture is to assist in change. Yet, by its nature, change is often disruptive – which means that many types of cultural problems may arise, for a wide variety of reasons, including:

- EA is all about exposing problems
- EA is all about exposing mistakes
- EA is all about bridging barriers, silos and fiefdoms

- EA is all about the benefit to the whole rather than the individual part

Many people and groups will not like any of this... It seems that people don't resist change as such, but do resist being changed – especially if the change doesn't seem to benefit them or their team. Without appropriate attention to the cultural aspects of enterprise-architecture, people are likely to resist any architectural change – and often fiercely so. If this is not respected, there is a high risk that EA efforts can create unwanted, unexpected and potentially disastrous side-effects. At the least, this has a high potential to waste effort, money and time. Hence the reason why culture is a Critical Success Factor in enterprise-architecture.

Enterprise-architecture should *not* attempt to change the culture of an organisation: that is not its role at all. Yet in order to succeed, EA needs to become embedded in the culture of the organisation: it *needs* those changes to happen. Part of this should arise from the communication strategy above; but it also involves understanding the relationships between people, and between groups of people, and understanding and respecting their needs, desires, hopes and fears – their motivation.

Hence this part of the PEAF products, to focus on those issues, and identify the skills and behaviours that enterprise-architects will need to express, in order to do the required work.

As with all architecture, we cannot begin to change anything unless we seek to understand it first. And often, merely seeking to understand other people's and departments' points of view and why they think and say what they do can reap huge architectural and other benefits.

For example, to understand people and groups in an organisation, we must consider the following areas:

- *Background* – Where did they come from? What have been their successes and failures? What paths have they walked down and what have they seen on their life's journey so far?
- *Beliefs* – What do they believe in? Survival of the fittest? Meritocracy? Democracy? Dictatorships, Socialism, Capitalism?
- *Experience* – What do they know? What do they not know? Is there a gap in their knowledge that they are hiding? What can they do? What can they not do? Are they adequately trained to do what they need to do?

- *Motivation* – What drives them to do what they do? What motivates their decisions?
- *Behaviour* – What types of behaviour do they exhibit?

We also need to watch for and document any divisive traits, such as 'style over substance', bullying, information-hiding and other related problems. Again, addressing these is *not* the responsibility of enterprise-architecture, but the fact of identifying them within any part of the organisation can help other groups such as HR and organisational-change to resolve them.

Relationships and mutual responsibilities between business units and management is another key area where the culture-aspects of EA efforts can deliver great dividends. The PEAF Culture product here provides checklists and other advice on how to identify what people and their business-units do, how they do it, and how this work relates to that of others.

Two other examples addressed in the Culture product are about relationships between management and workforce, and between IT and 'the business'. The product includes checklists and other exploratory notes on typical differences between management and workers, regarding:

- *Personal motivation* – short-term versus long-term
- *Career outlook* – mobility versus commitment to a single organisation
- *Financial motivation* – alignment of bonuses etc to short-term versus long-term

Although the same behaviour is evidenced by other parts of the organisation, IT units seem especially prone to seeing themselves as 'special and different' relative to everyone else: hence the all-too-common tendency to talk about IT versus 'the business' – in other words, everyone else. The Culture product provides another set of checklists to address this, in particular regarding:

- Characteristics
- Maturity of disciplines
- Strategic volatility and focus
- Tactical volatility and focus
- Re-use
- Control mechanisms and their effects
- Control-mechanism defence tactics

Another section of the Culture product explores the relationships between enterprise-architecture and change-projects, and the roles of architects, analysts, project-managers and others in relation to functional and 'non-functional' (qualitative) requirements and the resultant project-plans.

Skills and responsibilities

The other part of the Relationships product in the Culture section provides a list of the skills and resources required to prepare, implement and operate enterprise-architecture. Job Descriptions and Terms of Reference are provided for key individuals and groups.

The key players involved in enterprise-architecture include:

Boards:

- Board of Directors (BOD)
- Strategic Investment Board (SIB)
- Enterprise Architecture Review Board (EARB)
- Enterprise Architecture Project Board (EAPB)
- Unions, regulators and other 'external' bodies

Groups:

- Executive Management
- Business Departments
- Strategic Planning
- Project Personnel
- Human Resources (HR)
- Information Technology (IT)
- Employees
- Users
- 'Anyone'

Individuals:

- Enterprise-Architect – EA Preparation and Implementation
- Enterprise Architect – EA Operation
- Solution Architect
- Vendor
- Provider (for EA modelling)
- Subject Matter Expert (for EA modelling)
- Modeller (for EA modelling)

- Owner (for EA modelling)

As can be seen above, there are two distinct types of enterprise-architect role. 'EA Preparation and Implementation' is the focus of external consultants, who guide and mentor the initial EA effort. Most of the 'EA Operation' work, though, will usually need to be done by permanent members of staff, particularly those who have built up large social-networks within the organisation, and are personally familiar with the points of leverage and 'danger-areas' within the organisation's culture. The Culture product describes the respective job-descriptions under the following headings:

- *Purpose* – EA-practice development, EA operation etc
- *Focus* – communication, mentoring, planning or governance
- *Works with* – board, executive, strategy team or review
- *Typical duties* – in Prepare phase, Implement phase and Operate phase
- *Required experience* – frameworks, communication, negotiation, technologies and verticals, etc
- *Terms of employment* – consultant or permanent

Whether in an 'internal' or 'external' role, the skillsets needed for all types of enterprise-architecture work are much the same. The Culture product summarises the required skills and behaviours under the following headings:

Traits:

- Pragmatic
- Enthusiastic
- Agnostic
- Articulate
- Persistent
- Strategic
- Altruistic
- Diplomatic
- Open
- Generalist

Behaviours:

- Persuade
- Learn
- Investigate
- Abstract

- Expose
- Facilitate
- Lead

The Culture product also includes suggested Terms of Reference for the key governance-bodies – in other words, their respective 'job descriptions'.

Application

- What proportion of your time do you spend on the 'people-stuff' of enterprise-architecture – communicating and negotiating with the architecture's stakeholders – rather than the definitions, drawings and designs? To what extent *is* the architecture about people, rather than those visible artefacts of architecture? In essence, how important are those cultural concerns not just to the 'doing' of enterprise-architecture, but also to its overall success?

- To what extent – if at all – do your existing EA frameworks acknowledge the importance of organisational culture and the 'people-stuff'? What practical guidance – if any – do they provide in addressing those issues? What do you learn from that comparison, and how would you apply it in your EA practice?

- What skills, behaviours and character-traits do you currently look for in your enterprise-architects? Reviewing the descriptions above, what might you need to change? And by what means might you create those changes, in your other enterprise-architects, and in yourself?

PRODUCTS: MODELS

Summary

Models are perhaps the most visible products of any enterprise-architecture work – yet they're far more than just 'pretty pictures'. This section of PEAF provides practical detail on how the various model-types should be structured and used, why an EA toolset that's purpose-built for the task is so important in practice, and how to select one that matches the organisation's EA-maturity.

Details

The Model section of PEAF outlines the main artefact of an enterprise-architecture initiative – the EA Model. This section is made up of the following products:

- Metamodel
- Tool Rationale
- Tool Requirements
- Tool Vendors
- Tool Scores

Whilst people are the key to the success of enterprise-architecture, the EA Model forms the backbone of the architecture initiative, as it is the main repository of information about the organisation, its objectives, goals, targets and strategies, and one of the key means by which people communicate with each other about architectural issues.

The model is not solely for use by an elite group of individuals. The more people use it, and the more people contribute to it, the more benefit the organisation will attain.

Note that although it's common to talk about 'models', there is and should be only one actual model in an enterprise-architecture, as represented by the contents of the repository. In effect, all other 'models' are views into this one core model, as selected by context, scope, point in time (current, future, intermediate) and so on. Proliferation of separate, uncontrolled uncoordinated models – as often occurs without a managed enterprise-architecture – will represent a serious risk and significant Enterprise Debt.

Metamodel

This product details a high level Metamodel to describe entities or 'things' that an organisation wants to collect information about, and the relationships that can exist between those entities.

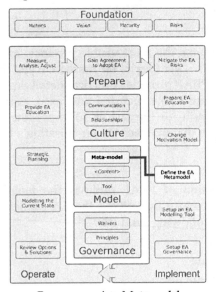

Processes using Metamodel

The Metamodel product within the Model section is used in the 'Define the EA Metamodel' tasks within the *Implement* phase.

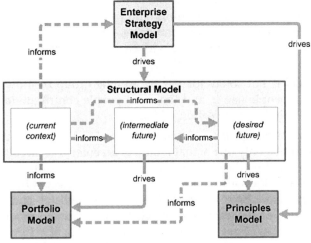

Overview of PEAF metamodel

The PEAF metamodel is a 'starter set' of predefined architectural entities. It can be used as-is, but would usually be amended or extended during the 'Define EA Metamodel' tasks, to match the specific needs and nature of the organisation. It can even be replaced altogether if a preferred or existing Metamodel is already in use. The point is that, wherever practicable, enterprise models should be based on the same underlying metamodel, to assist in consistency and communication across the enterprise.

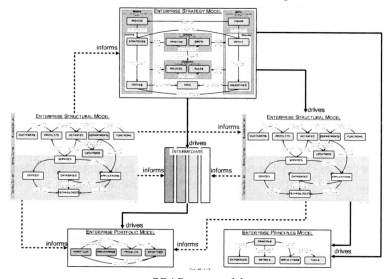

PEAF metamodel

Ideally, it should be possible to fit the core metamodel onto a single page, as shown for the PEAF Metamodel.

The PEAF Metamodel has four main components:

- Enterprise Strategy Model
- Enterprise Structural Model
- Enterprise Portfolio Model
- Enterprise Principles Model

The **Enterprise Strategy Model** captures vision, mission, goals, objectives and tactics of the enterprise, and key relationships between them. It is subdivided into the following groups:

- *Ends* – What the organisation wants to achieved (What).
- *Means* – How the organisation will achieve its Ends (How).
- *Drivers* – What is driving the Means to be defined (Why).
- *Guidance* – What will guide decisions and change.

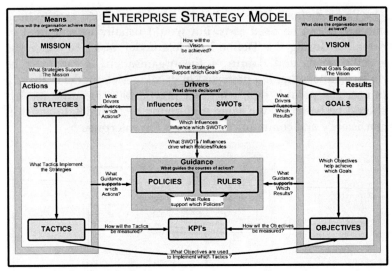

PEAF metamodel: Enterprise Strategy Model

This part of the metamodel is based on the international-standard Business Motivation Model. The initial entities within each of these groups are as follows:

Ends:

- *Vision* – A statement about the future state of the enterprise, without regard to how it is to be achieved.
- *Goal* – Statement about a state or condition of the enterprise to be brought about or sustained through appropriate means.
- *Objective* – Statement of a specific time-targeted, measurable, attainable target that an enterprise seeks to meet in order to achieve its Goals.

Means:

- *Mission* – The ongoing operational activity of an enterprise.
- *Strategy* – Course of action that is one component of a plan for a Mission.
- *Tactic* – Course of action that represents part of the detailing of Strategies.

Drivers:

- *Influence* – An act, process, or power of producing an effect without apparent exertion of tangible force or direct exercise of command, and often without deliberate effort or intent.

- *Strength* – An assessment that an Influence indicates an advantage or area of excellence within an enterprise that can impact its employment of Means or achievement of Ends.
- *Weakness* – An assessment that an Influence indicates an area of inadequacy within an enterprise that can impact its employment of Means or achievement of Ends.
- *Opportunity* – An assessment that an Influence can have a favourable impact on its employment of Means or achievement of Ends.
- *Threat* – An assessment that an Influence can have an unfavourable impact on its employment of Means or achievement of Ends.

Guidance:

- *Business Rule* – Influences or guides business behavior, in support of Business Policy.
- *Business Policy* – Guides the enterprise.

As described above, this part of the metamodel can be amended in accordance with the organisation's needs.

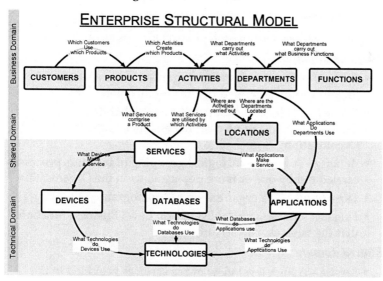

PEAF metamodel: Enterprise Structural Model

The **Enterprise Structural Model** captures information about the 'things' that make up the enterprise and how they are related. It models the enterprise from a structural perspective. The 'starter-set' of entities here are those best suited to describe connections and dependencies between IT and other parts of the business – the most common issues where organisations begin their enterprise-architecture efforts.

This metamodel would be used to depict the structures of the enterprise at different points in time:

- *Current* – Models the structure of an enterprise as it exists at present.
- *Target* (desired future) – Models the structure of the enterprise at some point in the future. Its content tends to be much less defined than the Current Model because it is aspirational.
- *Intermediate* – Models the structure of the enterprise at various points in time between the Current and Target states.

The graphic above illustrates the Current Metamodel in terms of entities and relationships.

It is further conceptually divided into :-

- *Business Domain* – The things relating to the business.
- *Technical Domain* – The things relating to technology.
- *Shared Domain* – The things which sit between the business and technology.

The initial entities within each of these groups are as follows:

Business domain:

- *Customer* – Some one, group, organisation or agency which utilises products created by the Organisation
- *Product* – A Physical product or service that the Organisation provides (for cost or no cost) to customers outside of the Organisation
- *Activity* – A high Level logical grouping of business processes carried out by one or more departments in the Organisation
- *Department* – The organisation's Organogram
- *Function* – A hierarchical list of Top Level Business functions that the business carries out.

Shared domain:

- *Service* – A high level view of the services provided to the business from IS
- *Location* – The physical locations the Organisation uses

Technical domain:

- *Application* – The main applications in use at the Organisation

- *Database* – The main database in use at IS, either related to applications or standalone
- *Device* – A logical name for a generic piece of hardware provided as or part of a service to the business, such as Tablet, Blackberry, Plotter, etc
- *Technology* – A logical name for a generic piece of technology, such as Windows, Coldfusion, Oracle, Tibco, Websphere

This part of the metamodel will definitely need to be augmented as the organisation extends its enterprise-architecture effort to cover more than the classic 'business/IT divide'.

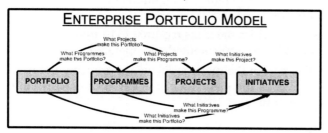

PEAF metamodel: Enterprise Portfolio Model

The **Enterprise Portfolio Model** captures portfolios, programmes, projects and initiatives that are born out of analysing the Current, Target and Intermediate states, and defines what needs to be done to advance the enterprise from the Current to the Target, through the Intermediate models.

The initial entities in this part of the metamodel are as follows:

- *Portfolio* – A grouping of Programmes, Projects and Initiatives
- *Programme* – A grouping of Projects and Initiatives
- *Project* – A grouping of Initiatives
- *Initiative* – An item of work.

This part of the metamodel would probably not need any change.

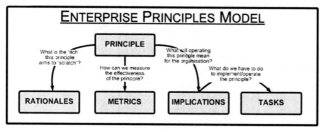

PEAF metamodel: Principles

The **Enterprise Principles Model** captures the Principles that will be used to guide the work defined in the Portfolio model.

The initial entities in this part of the metamodel are as follows:

- *Principle* – An expression of intent for strategic benefit.
- *Rationale* – Highlights the Business benefits of adhering to the principle, using business terminology.
- *Metric* – The measures that must be in place in order to monitor whether the positive results that each principle is meant to achieve are being achieved
- *Implication* – Highlight the requirements, both for the Business and IS, for carrying out the principle
- *Tasks* – Specifies the tasks required to be undertaken for the principle to be implemented and operated.

Again, this part of the metamodel would probably not need much if any change as the maturity of the enterprise-architecture effort develops over time.

Model-content

From the end-user's perspective, the main artefact of enterprise-architecture is the model and its model-content – 'models' – that allow architecture-information to be gathered, updated, viewed, analysed and applied.

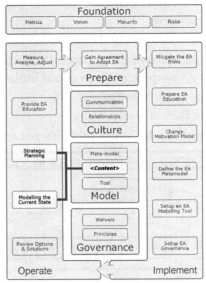

Processes using Model-content

Model-content is used mainly in the 'Modelling the Current State' and 'Strategic Planning' tasks in the *Operate* phase. All model-content should be based on the EA metamodel.

Tools

Wherever practicable, the model-content should be developed via a purpose-built toolset for EA modelling. Most of the products in the Models section relate to the rationale for using a purpose-built toolset, and criteria and further guidance on tools selection.

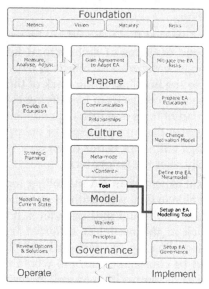

Processes using Tools

These Tools products of the Model section are used in the 'Setup an EA Modelling Tool' tasks within the *Implement* phase.

The first Tools product explains what an EA modelling tool does, and why it is so necessary. Themes and issues discussed include the accelerating rate of change faced by most organisations, and increasing complexity of organisational 'ecosystems' of suppliers, customers, outsourcers, media, legislation, competition and the like. Although enterprise-architecture can often start out small and simple, the pace and scale of change and complexity is such that some kind of purpose-built tool soon becomes essential. The point at which an EA becomes mandatory tends to be reached a lot sooner than organisations realise.

In essence there are three fundamental types of information to be maintained and managed in an EA tool:

- *Entities* – the 'things' that you gather information about such as Objectives, Business processes, Applications, Goals, Locations, Departments, Databases.
- *Relationships* – the 'linkages' between the entities, such as relating Business Processes to Departments or applications
- *Views* – the 'diagrams' which are illustrations of one or more Entities and one or more Relationships drawn in a particular kind of notation.

It's important to note that these should not be regarded simply as a kind of catalogue of 'items of architectural interest'. A phrase often heard amongst enterprise-architects is that "the value is not in the boxes but in the lines": keeping track of things is useful, yet the real business value comes from identifying the leverage-points amongst the myriad of links and interdependencies between those things. This reiterates the core principle of enterprise-architecture that, overall, things will work better when they work together, on purpose, especially over the longer term.

Another important aspect of an EA modelling tool is *time*. It must be possible to be able to deal with entities over their lifetime, often through multiple versions and multiple views. It is also important to be able to look at the model at different levels of detail or 'granularity', depending on the task in hand. The relationships displayed should be consistent with the whole model both from the point of view of decomposition as well as abstraction.

To explain this, three categories of EA toolsets are described:

- *Ordinary office software-tools* – for example Microsoft Excel with Visio or Powerpoint for diagrams
- *Office-tools with database*
- *Purpose-built tool* with customised shared-repository

For each of these, the Tools Rationale product summarises typical training-requirements, entity and relationship management in diagrams, consistency, cost, ability to use and share the model, and effort needed to maintain the model over time. In both the 'office-software' categories, low cost and familiarity of use are real advantages in the earliest stages, but will rapidly hit up against very steep curves of diminishing-returns. Although it's true that some EA tools do come with very high price-tags, those are primarily designed for use in large corporations, where in practice they are by no means as expensive as they might at first seem. And given that some EA tools are low or even no cost, it seems wise to move over to a proper tool as soon as practicable.

Another question addressed is whether a CMDB (Configuration Management Database, for IT systems and suchlike) can be used as an EA toolset. The short answer is it rarely does that job well: it can be very useful when used in conjunction with an EA toolset, but not as a substitute for it – the context, scope and purpose, and even the entities and attributes, are usually too different to do so.

The next product in the section, Tool Requirements, details a set of suggested requirement-criteria for the selection of a single tool or toolset for EA modelling. These requirements, and the matching review-checklist for vendor demonstrations, are organised under the following headings:

- Importing
- Exporting
- Relationships
- User Interface / Ease of use
- Diagrams / Views
- Impact Analysis
- Metamodel
- Target and Intermediate Models
- Management
- Supplementary Questions
- Expected Views
- Expected Dashboards

The final two products in the Models section – Tool Vendors and Tool Scores – provide summaries of the offerings of most of the EA tool vendors presently in the marketplace, and present the vendors' own scoring of their offerings relative to the criteria listed in the PEAF Tool Requirements product. Note that all of the information these products was supplied by vendors themselves: accuracy and correctness of the information rests solely with the individual companies concerned. It should probably not be used as the basis for any purchase-decisions without careful review in the respective business-context, but in keeping with the pragmatic principles of PEAF, it does provide a useful springboard to do so: "everything you need to get started, and nothing you don't".

Application

- What metamodels - if any – are provided by your existing EA frameworks?

- If none are provided, how do you link all of your models together? How do you ensure consistency and common meaning across the many aspects of the enterprise?

- If one or more metamodels are provided, what scope do they cover? Do they only describe IT, or the flow of business-processes? Do they include the human side of business, linking back to the motivations and values that drive the enterprise? If they don't describe the human side of business, how do you keep everything on track to business purpose?

- What model-content do you present to your architecture-clients? And why? Who is the end-user for each type of diagram? What is its practical purpose – its business-value?

- How do you develop the diagrams and other artefacts of architecture? What tools and techniques do you use? Why those tools and techniques, rather than any other?

- How do you ensure that each diagram and document represents a view into a *single* model of the enterprise as a whole? How do you prevent fragmentation of that single model into a myriad of misleading mixed interpretations?

- What means – if any – does your existing toolset for architecture-modelling provide in keeping all the information up to date? How do you keep track of versions, revisions, updates? And who has the responsibility and authority to keep track of all those versions?

- As you develop the architecture-maturity, you will also need to grow the maturity of the toolset you use for architecture-modelling. By what means will you assess the capabilities of your existing toolset? How will you identify what facilities need to change? What support do your existing EA frameworks provide for this procurement process?

PRODUCTS: GOVERNANCE

Summary

EA acts as the glue between strategy and execution: assisting in governance and guidance of organisational change is perhaps the real core of enterprise-architecture. To aid in this, PEAF provides explanations and templates for two key types of EA 'products': guiding-principles, and waivers that are used to document any changes to Enterprise Debt.

Details

The Governance set of products address the quality control that is needed to ensure that agreed principles, policies and standards are followed, or, if not, that the impacts, risks and implications of not doing so are costed, understood, accepted and managed.

These products form two groups: documentation of principles for design and governance; and 'waivers' that document unavoidable deviations from those principles, and what to do to mitigate the resultant risks.

Principles

The Principles product details a set of widely accepted principles that apply to and are relevant within most organisations.

As with the Metamodel, this is essentially a 'starter-set'. As work progresses, these principles should be augmented with principles arising from considering the Enterprise Strategy Model and other aspects of the organisation's own needs and context.

The purpose of these principles is not to constrain, but to provide a broad cultural framework in which work will be carried out. A principle should be never regarded as a hard-and-fast rule, but instead as a clear guideline to aid in decision-making. In every case, principles should be linked back to enterprise vision and goals, providing a clear business rationale for the respective principle.

The Principles product of the Governance section is used mainly in the 'Setup EA Governance' tasks in the *Implement* phase, and in the 'Review Options & Solutions' tasks in the *Operate* phase.

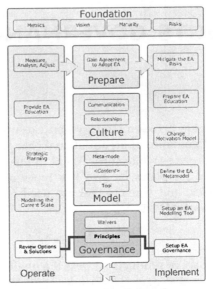

Processes using Principles

In the PEAF product, each item in the 'starter-set' of principles is described in a consistent way, using the following structure:

- *Name* – Represents the essence of the rule as well as being easy to remember.
- *Statement* – Succinctly and unambiguously communicates the fundamental rule.
- *Rationale* – Highlights the *business benefits* of adhering to the principle, using business terminology.
- *Implications* – Highlight the requirements for carrying out the principle - in terms of resources, costs, and activities/tasks.
- *Metrics* – Lists the measures that must be in place in order to monitor whether the positive results that each principle is meant to achieve are being achieved.

The metrics given for each principle are essential because they identify how well that principle is achieving its desired result. It is also important to distinguish between 'raw' metrics versus the more meaningful 'derived' metrics for which the raw-metrics are the inputs. Metrics need to focus on outcomes, not inputs: for example, there is little value in merely counting the number of waivers issued, without further derived-analysis, because that is like measuring how fast we are pumping water, not how much water we are pumping.

60

Example principle

- Name: Principle E1: Apply Principles Universally
- Statement: These principles apply to all parts of the organisation.
- Rationale: If parts of the organisation are exempt from these principles, this will undermine and reduce the benefits gained to an unacceptable level.
- Implications: Parts of the enterprise may react negatively and resist the removal of the 'flexibility' to pick and choose which principles to adopt; all change initiatives will be reviewed for their compliance with the principles; an unresolved conflict with a principle will be resolved by issuing a Waiver which will then be analysed, costed and managed.
- Metrics (raw):
  - Percent of Initiatives that have been examined for compliance with the principles.
  - Per project: Number of waivers issued
  - Per project: Number of waiver issues
  - Per project: Total Cost of waiver issues
  - Per project: Number of waiver risks
  - Per project: Total impact cost of waiver risks
  - Per project: Number Waivers avoided
- Metrics (derived):
  - Total number of live waivers
  - Total number of waivers issued
  - Total number of waivers closed
  - Total number of waiver issues
  - Total cost of waiver issues
  - Total number of waiver risks
  - Total impact cost of waiver risks
  - Total number waivers avoided (and at which level)

The full 'starter-set' of principles described within the Principles product are as follows:

Enterprise-architecture principles

- Principle E1: Apply Principles Universally
- Principle E2: Proactive Business Leadership
- Principle E3: Recognise Responsibilities

- Principle E4: Manage Enterprise Debt Value (EDV)
- Principle E5: Manage Enterprise Debt Ratio (EDR)
- Principle E6: Plan Ahead and Organise
- Principle E7: Relationships & Traceability
- Principle E8: Think Strategically
- Principle E9: Be Architecture Centric
- Principle E10: Business Continuity
- Principle E11: Compliance
- Principle E12: Have a Sound Business case
- Principle E13: Consolidate
- Principle E14: Avoid Under/Over Engineering
- Principle E15: Be Service Oriented
- Principle E16: Reduce Manual Processes
- Principle E17: Open Integration
- Principle E18: Reuse
- Principle E19: Explain Decisions

Applications principles

- Principle A1: Ease-of-Use
- Principle A2: Replace Legacy Systems Appropriately
- Principle A3: Common Use Applications
- Principle A4: Buy (for reuse) Before Build
- Principle A5: Application Security

Data/information principles

- Principle D1: Data is an Asset
- Principle D2: Data is Shared
- Principle D3: Data is Accessible
- Principle D4: Common Vocabulary
- Principle D5: Data Security

Technology principles

- Principle T1: Increase Technology Independence
- Principle T2: Reduce Technology Diversity
- Principle T3: Increase Technology Interoperability

Within the Principles product, two final sections map each of the 'starter-set' principles to respective Enterprise Goals (Efficiency, Effectiveness, Agility, Durability), and to the tasks that need to be undertaken in order to be able to enact the principle.

Waivers

This product details the information that should be captured to understand when Enterprise Debt is being created and the impact of that debt so that informed decisions can be made.

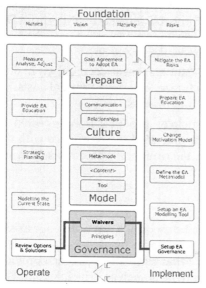

Processes using Waivers

The Waivers product of the Governance section is used mainly in the 'Setup EA Governance' tasks in the *Implement* phase, and in the 'Review Options & Solutions' tasks in the *Operate* phase.

The product is a suggested template to be used to document non-compliance (or, in some cases, re-compliance) with the intended architecture – in other words issues that could increase (or reduce) Enterprise Debt. The template presents its instructions, guidance and explanations in the following format:

- *Waiver Summary* – provides an overview of the waiver, why it is being issued, associated costs, the decision taken, and the reasons for that decision.
- *Cause of Non-Compliance* – describes what prevents compliance at present, such as costs, people, time, scope or process.
- *Non-Compliance Issues* that arise through non-compliance – for each issue, summarises the issue itself, actions to be taken, expected costs, target completion-date and owner of the action.

- *Non-Compliance Risks,* or risks that arise through the non-compliance – for each, summarises the effect of the risk, its probable time-horizon, probability, impact on occurrence, mitigating actions and costs, target-date and action-owner.
- *Total Cost of Non-Compliance* – for each issue or risk, summarises probable impacts on Enterprise Debt, in terms of capital-costs, revenue costs, people required, and effects on schedules, timescales and scope.
- *Remediation* – summarises tasks required in order to be compliant in future, in terms of capital-costs, revenue-costs, people, time and process.

As with the Principles product, it is expected that the Waiver template could be amended in accordance with the organisation's needs. However, the content provided has been sufficient as-is for many PEAF licensees.

Application

- What practical support – if any – do your existing EA frameworks provide for the day-to-day needs of architecture governance? What templates does each provide for key governance-artefacts such as Principles and Waivers?
- Waivers (or 'dispensations') provide a key means to document unavoidable deviations from intended design – in other words, the pragmatics of real-world architecture. What information needs to be built in to each Waiver to ensure that each decision is revisited and reviewed as appropriate at some future time? Who is responsible for keeping track of Waivers as they become due for review? Who actions those reviews? When? Why? How?
- Who is the end-customer for each documented Principle or Waiver? How would they use this information? How do you ensure that this information is used appropriately in the organisation's decision-making?

PROCESS: START

Summary

The Start point in PEAF represents a decision by someone to start off an EA effort for the first time. This starts off the PEAF cycle of EA processes.

Details

Get started

The Start icon shown on the PEAF graphic is neither a Product nor a Process as such, but more a decision or commitment to use and apply enterprise-architecture within the organisation. Everything flows from that one decision to get started.

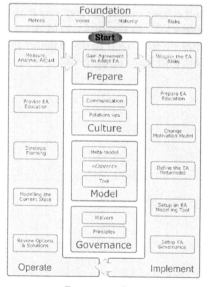

Processes: Start

The Start decision leads immediately to the *Prepare* phase in the PEAF cycle of processes, and the 'Gain Agreement to Adopt EA' process and its tasks within that phase.

The Start icon is also a useful reminder that this *is* a cycle, not a 'once-off' project. Completion of the 'Measure, Analyse, Adjust' process in the *Operate* phase – the last part of the PEAF cycle, used to aid in continuous-improvement of the EA capability – is also, by definition, the start of the next cycle.

Application

- How did you get started in enterprise-architecture? What was the trigger that got you started on this journey?
- What did you need in place before you could start? Before you did get started, what was it that seemed to prevent you from getting started? What organisational and other barriers did you need to surmount?
- How did – or would – the organisation get started in enterprise-architecture? What needs to happen to break free from the usual inertia against starting in anything new?
- Once you've gotten started, what do you need in order to ensure that you don't stop? Whenever the architecture-capability itself comes up for review – as it always will at some point, especially in the real-world pressures of everyday business – what do you need to do in order to ensure that you can keep going, and keep adding value to the enterprise?

PROCESS: PREPARE

Summary

The 'Prepare' phase of the PEAF architecture-cycle enacts a key part of governance, confirming the overall business-case for each item of EA work, and ensuring alignment with the architectural and other aims of the organisation.

Details

The 'Prepare' phase

The Prepare phase of PEAF is concerned with setting out the business case for starting or renewing an EA initiative and gaining the required remit, budget and resources.

The resulting EA Implementation Plan is born out of considering the Maturity model, deciding upon the level that an organisation currently maps to, the level that it wishes to map to, and the timescales in which it would like to make the transition.

This phase has a single process:

• Gain Agreement to Adopt EA

The product-set for this phase consists of a document describing the process, and an example project-plan in Microsoft Project file-format, to guide the first pass through the process. (The process would change somewhat in the second and subsequent iterations through the PEAF architecture-development cycle, with a focus on maturity-review and enhancement rather than initial setup.)

Gain agreement to adopt EA

This process is concerned with setting out to executives and others the raison d'être for adopting EA, and obtaining the necessary support and funding to proceed. It defines the vision for EA, and identifies the risks involved, as indicated by the organisation's current maturity of the organisation with regard to EA. Having agreed how mature the organisation is, how mature it wishes to be and how the risks will be mitigated, a plan can then be drawn up to allow the board to decide whether or not to proceed to implementation and operation.

The process is similar in the second and subsequent cycles: the main difference is that, rather than doing the initial maturity-evaluation from scratch, as described below, the assessment builds on the maturity-review from the 'Measure, Analyse & Adjust' process at the end of the previous *Operate* phase. The purpose in this later case is to report back to the board on progress to date, and verify funding to continue the work.

Timescales will vary for different enterprises depending on their size and complexity, but this work would typically be completed within ten to thirty days.

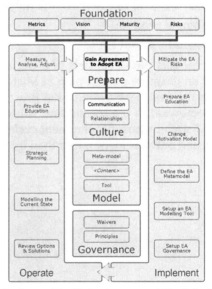

Products used in Gain Agreement To Adopt EA

The main PEAF *Products* used in this process are Metrics, Vision, Maturity, Risks and Communication.

In terms of the 'players' listed in the Relationships product in the Culture set, the key *Actors* in this process are Board of Directors, Executive Management and Enterprise Architect.

The key steps can be summarised as follows.

Choose Framework: The Executive Management and Board of Directors agree to explore EA. Either they, or, more usually, a delegate, will identify suitable EA frameworks to assess.

If PEAF is selected as a framework to use, Executive Management will assign the role of Enterprise Architect. This person will then undergo PEAF training, and train other stakeholders in PEAF as appropriate.

Agree Vision: The Enterprise Architect will develop a vision for EA, particularly in terms of future maturity in EA practice, and present it to others for review and subsequent sign-off by the Executive.

Consider Maturity: The Enterprise Architect will create the EA Maturity Model, and identify the 'current state' and 'desired target state' for the current iteration of the PEAF-cycle.

The Enterprise Architect will create the EA Risk Register, and identify mitigation strategies for each risk in the register.

The Enterprise Architect will also identify and specify the metrics required for monitoring of EA.

All of these items will be presented to others for review and for sign-off by the Executive.

Plan Implementation: The Enterprise Architect will develop an Implementation Plan for EA. This will then be presented to others for review, and sign-off by the Executive.

Get Agreement: The Enterprise Architect and Executive work together to develop the formal business-case for EA, and present it to the Board for review and final approval.

Application

- What do you need to do to get approval to start or continue the enterprise-architecture capability? From whom do you need this approval, and how, and why?
- What do you need to do in order to prepare for this approval-process? What information and other evidence do you need?

- Within an organisational setting, you will need funding, access to resources, the right people, the right skills, and some of form of authority to proceed; to have an impact on change, you will need your governance-processes to have serious backing from above. Yet what else do you need to get started, or to keep going? Who are the other stakeholders in the architecture? How would you gain their engagement in the overall process?
- What support – if any – do your existing EA frameworks provide in this process? If none, how *do* you get started?

PROCESS: IMPLEMENT

Summary

This section of the architecture-cycle implements the changes within the organisation that are needed to establish and operate the EA capability. These tasks focus on key themes such as communication, motivation, and setup for modelling to support decision-making. It's also important here to set up or verify appropriate governance for the required changes, and identify, monitor and mitigate the risks and opportunities that arise from it.

Details

The 'Implement' processes

The purpose of the PEAF *Implement* phase is to enact the changes and adjustments to the organisation that will be needed in order to utilise the enterprise-architecture.

The work to be done depends on the specific goals and timescales of the respective enterprise, as identified in the *Prepare* phase.

In essence, the implementation of the changes required to operate and gain the benefits of enterprise-architecture consist of minor adjustments to the existing structures and processes within the enterprise. It should not require installation of large numbers of people in teams, or adoption of a raft of new business-processes.

There is a natural tendency for people to want to go straight to the 'doing' of EA, but these are key tasks that cannot and must not be skipped-over or ignored. If this setup-work is not done, or not done well, any subsequent EA work is at risk of being of only very limited use, and is liable to die as 'shelfware' very quickly indeed.

This phase has six distinct processes that can occur in parallel:

- **Prepare EA Education**
- **Change Motivation Model**
- **Define the EA Metamodel**
- **Setup an EA Modelling Tool**
- **Setup EA Governance**
- **Mitigate the EA Risks**

71

The product-set for this phase consists of a document describing the processes, and an example project-plan in Microsoft Project file-format. (This example-plan assumes that the organisation is at level 1 in all areas of its EA maturity, and wishes to move to level 2 in all areas of maturity.) The detailed content of the project-plan actually used would be the output of the *Prepare*-phase planning.

Prepare EA education

This process creates materials required for ongoing, continuous education and two way communication about EA. It is concerned with educating people about enterprise-architecture in general, and about the organisation's EA framework in particular.

This process, together with provision of training and education in the *Operate* phase, is perhaps the most important of EA processes.

Communication and education is one of the keys to mitigating many of the risks associated with adoption of EA. For enterprise-architecture to be a success, good quality continuous education is mandatory. *If it is not done, or is done badly, the architecture initiative will fail.*

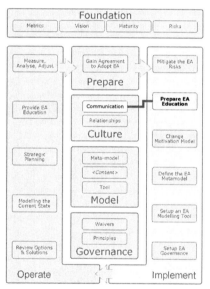

Products used in Prepare EA Education

The main PEAF *Products* used or referenced in this process are the Communication set.

The key *Actors* in this process are Board of Directors, Executive Management and Enterprise Architect.

The key steps can be summarised as follows.

Preparation: On receipt of the authorisation-to-proceed from the Executive, the Enterprise Architect identifies stakeholder-groups for enterprise-architecture, and creates, prepares or adapts suitable materials for EA training.

Initial Training: The Enterprise Architect will first run EA training for the Board of Directors and for the Executive. This is because, to succeed, the cultural-change for EA will usually need to be driven from the top of an organisation: its leaders must lead the EA effort by example.

Obtain Agreement on Communication Plan: During the initial training, the Enterprise Architect will also develop the overall EA Communication Plan. This will then be presented to others for review and for sign-off by the Executive.

Change motivation-model

One of the key concerns in enterprise-architecture is achieving an appropriate balance between short-term and long-term – yet most organisations' performance-schemes and motivation-models are strongly skewed towards the short-term. This process effects the cultural and human change necessary to bring about a more long term view of the management and direction of the organisation.

This is another Critical Success Factor for enterprise-architecture. The blunt fact is that it does not matter how many architectural principles, processes or models are adopted if the overall direction and management of the organisation are based upon motivation-structures that compromise its future in favour of short-term gains for individuals or individual units, rather than for the enterprise as a whole. Without these changes in place, the architecture will fail – and with it, ultimately, the entire organisation.

This part of the work is highly 'political', and obviously cannot be done by enterprise-architecture alone. However, the Enterprise Architect does need to ensure that these issues are resolved, and can play a key role in ensuring successful resolution by all parties.

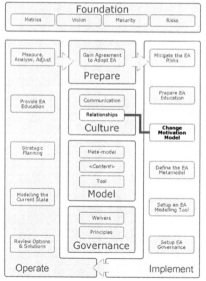

Products used in Change Motivation-Model

The main PEAF *Product* used or referenced within this process is Relationships.

The key *Actors* within this process are Board of Directors, Union, Employees, Executive Management, and HR.

The key steps can be summarised as follows.

Preparation: On receipt of authorisation-to-proceed, HR identifies suggested changes to the organisation's motivation-models. These are then presented to the Board of Directors and Executive Management for initial review and preliminary sign-off.

Consultation: HR then guides extensive consultation with Employees, Unions and the Executive. This will typically lead to an iterative cycle of updates, review, consultation and further updates, until overall agreement is reached. The final motivation-model is presented for final review and sign-off by the Board and all the stakeholders.

Implementation: On sign-off by the Board, HR implements the approved changes to the organisation's active motivation-model.

Define the EA metamodel

This process defines the metamodel to be used for gathering and analysing information stored in and by the EA modelling-tool.

Some EA modelling-tools have pre-installed metamodels; a few also do not enable editing of the metamodel. In such cases, this process may not be required. However, even if the only option is to use whatever metamodel that comes with the selected tool, it is still advisable to go through this process, to identify the entities, relationships and views that are important to the enterprise: a massive overly-detailed Metamodel can dilute the focus.

Note also the Structural Metamodel (as distinct from the Strategy, Portfolio and Principles domains) will necessarily be somewhat dependent on the process used for populating the current model, and the questions to be answered in and by that process.

Another focus or concern is that whatever initial metamodel is chosen, it will necessarily extend over time. Consideration should hence be given not only to the initial content of the metamodel, but also how it will change over time – hence, in turn, a probable need for an EA Metamodel change-roadmap.

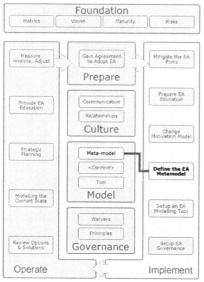

Products used in Define EA Metamodel

The main PEAF *Product* used or referenced within this process is Metamodel.

The key *Actors* within this process are Executive Management and Enterprise Architect.

The key steps can be summarised as follows.

Definition: The Executive Management, usually with assistance from the Enterprise Architect, identify and define the 'Important Questions' that underpin and guide sensemaking and decision-making in the organisation.

Guided by these 'Important Questions', the Enterprise Architect will develop definitions for the key entities and relations to be used within the initial and target Structural Metamodel, Strategy Metamodel, Portfolio Metamodel and Principles Metamodel, and for Views into the resultant model(s) that will then be used by the various stakeholders.

Obtain Sign-Off: On completion, the Enterprise Architect presents the metamodels to others for review and subsequent sign-off by the Executive.

Set up an EA modelling tool

This process addresses the procurement of tools or toolsets for EA modelling.

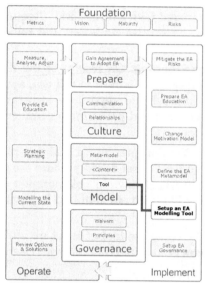

Products used in Set up EA Modelling Tool

Much of the information captured and maintained within this toolset will be used with, linked to or exchanged with other areas of the business such as portfolio planning, change-management, risk-management, configuration-management and the like. Hence due consideration must be given as to how the EA tool would fit in with the landscape of other tools utliised by the organisation.

The main PEAF *Product* used or referenced in this process is Tools.

The key *Actors* within this process are Vendors, EA Project Board, Enterprise Architect, Users, and IT.

The key steps can be summarised as follows.

Preparation: On receipt of authority-to-proceed from the EA Project Board, the Enterprise Architect will research a list of potential toolsets and their vendors, to develop the evaluation criteria and detailed requirements for a formal RFI (Request For Information) from the selected set of Vendors. This is passed to the EA Project Board for review and sign-off.

RFI (Request for Information): The Enterprise Architect sends the RFI to the selected Vendors. Their formal responses are evaluated by the EA Project Board, to select a shortlist. These Vendors are invited to demonstrate their respective toolsets, assessed against the final evaluation-criteria. The EA Project Board select a subset of Vendors to be issued with a formal RFP (Request For Proposal), developed by the Enterprise Architect, and reviewed by the EA Project Board.

RFP (Request for Proposal): On receipt of the RFP, the Vendors demonstrate the respective toolset in full use, applying the actual defined EA Metamodel and repository structures. This should lead to proof-of-concept and preliminary commercial negotiations with a final Vendor.

Installation: The Vendor presents a training-plan and system-configuration. The EA Project Board procure the required licenses and system hardware, if any. In collaboration the Vendor, the organisation's IT will set up any required hardware and software-configuration.

Training: Once the complete toolset is set up and configured, the Vendor will conduct out initial training with Users as required.

Set up EA governance

This process creates a set of enterprise-architecture principles, and puts in place the governance structures required to operate EA effectively.

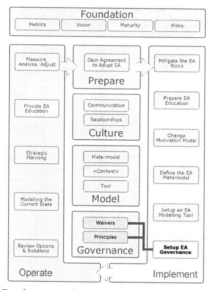

Products used in Set up EA Governance

The main PEAF *Products* used or referenced in this process are Principles and Waivers.

The key *Actors* in this process are Board of Directors, Executive Management, Enterprise Architect, Strategic Planning, Strategic Investment Board, EA Review Board, and Project Personnel.

The key steps can be summarised as follows.

Preparation: Given authority-to-proceed from the Executive, the Enterprise Architect identifies and defines terms-of-reference for the EA SIB (Strategic Investment Board) and EA Review Board; the process for 'Review Options & Solutions'; and the waiver-template and its associated processes. These are presented to others for review and subsequent sign-off by the Executive and Board. The Board of Directors then allocates budget for operational EA governance.

Formation: Together with Strategic Planning, the Enterprise Architect defines EA 'best practice' principles, aligned with strategic principles. The SIB and EARB are formed, in accordance with their respective terms-of-reference. A final governance review is conducted and signed-off by the Enterprise Architect, Strategic Planning, SIB and EARB, and Executive Management

Rollout: The Strategic Planning team will action any tasks arising from the review. The Enterprise Architect will then conduct EA governance training for Project Personnel.

Mitigate the EA risks

This process identifies and mitigates any risks associated with an EA initiative. This extends the work on risks previously carried out during the *Prepare* phase.

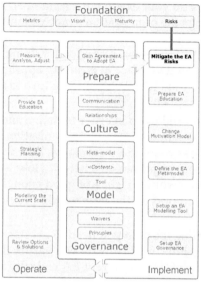

Products used in Mitigate EA Risks

The main PEAF *Product* used or referenced in this process is Risks.

The key *Actors* in this process are EA Project Board, Enterprise Architect, and Others.

The key steps can be summarised as follows.

Analyse: The Enterprise Architect prepares the initial set of enterprise-architecture risks. These risks are then reviewed and assessed by the EA Project Board during a workshop on EA risks.

Mitigate the Risks: The Enterprise Architect identifies appropriate mitigating actions for each of the reviewed risks. These actions are then passed to the respective other parties to resolve.

Application

- What support do your existing frameworks provide in preparing for EA education? What might you need to do for this in addition to the practical tasks described in PEAF?

- In what ways do your existing EA frameworks explain the need to change the organisation's motivation-models to enhance overall enterprise effectiveness? What practical support do the frameworks provide for doing this? What difficulties would you face in ensuring appropriate changes to the motivation-models? Who can you turn to for help in making this happen?

- What do you need to do in order to define and implement an appropriate metamodel for your organisation? If your existing EA frameworks provide a metamodel, how would you tailor it to match your organisation's needs? How will you know when the framework is right – or good enough to get started with? What support do the frameworks provide for this process?

- What modelling tools do you need to get started with enterprise-architecture? How do you ensure that the toolset is the right match for your current EA maturity and needs?

- What do you need to do to embed enterprise-architecture within your organisation's governance-processes? How would you ensure that EA governance has the 'teeth' that it needs?

- What practical processes do you need to go through in order to identify and mitigate the risks to your EA? With whom would you do this, and via what means? What opportunities do each of these risks show you, in terms of how to do your EA differently, or to do it better?

PROCESS: OPERATE

Summary

This section of the PEAF architecture-cycle applies the same EA principles to change-projects whilst the options for the respective needs and solutions are assessed and developed. These processes ensure that appropriate communication, modelling, governance and alignment to organisational strategy all take place as required, so as to minimise and, wherever practicable, reduce the present and future risks and costs represented by Enterprise Debt.

Details

The 'Operate' processes

The Operate Phase of PEAF enacts the day-to-day processes of 'doing' enterprise-architecture.

These processes are usually much the same for all enterprises, although they may change somewhat, dependent on the structure and needs of the specific organisation.

This phase includes five processes:

- **Provide EA Education**
- **Modelling the Current State**
- **Strategic Planning**
- **Review Options & Solutions**
- **Measure, Analyse & Adjust**

All five processes may be run in parallel; however, the 'Measure, Analyse & Adjust' process also typically marks the end of an architecture cycle.

The product-set for this phase consists of a document describing the processes, and an example project-plan in Microsoft Project file-format for the 'Strategic Planning' and 'Modelling the Current State' processes. (No example project-plan is provided for the other three processes, either because the practical details depend primarily on the local context, or, in the case of 'Measure, Analyse & Adjust', need to be dovetailed into the organisation's existing project-lifecycle processes.)

Provide EA education

This process takes the materials and communication plan that were created in the *Implementation* phase, and executes the plan.

Coupled with the preparation work in the *Implementation* phase, this is perhaps the most important of all the EA processes.

Communication and education are some of the keys to mitigating many of the risks associated with the adoption of EA. As was described earlier, good quality continuous education is mandatory if the enterprise-architecture is to be a success. *If this education is not done, or is done badly, the EA initiative will fail.*

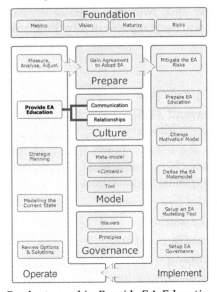

Products used in Provide EA Education

The main PEAF *Products* used or referenced in this process are Communications and Relationships.

The key *Actors* within this process are Executive Management, Enterprise Architect, Business Department, and Anyone.

The key steps can be summarised as follows.

Provide Education: Once the *Operation* phase begins, the Enterprise Architect will:

- Run EA training sessions for Business Departments.
- Provide regular updates to Executive Management.

- Present regular 'roadshows' on enterprise-architecture themes for Business Departments and Executive Management.
- Provide a regular 'surgery' on specific enterprise-architecture issues for project-members and others affected by EA matters.

The 'surgery' and executive updates would typically be held on a monthly basis, whilst the 'roadshows' are more likely to be run at quarterly intervals.

Education and training would typically take two main forms:

- Formal classroom based information and knowledge transfer.
- Informal discussions, workshops and round tables.

Classroom-based education is often the most practicable means to present and transfer the core information and knowledge about enterprise-architecture – what it is and how it works in practice, and the mechanics of how to adopt and operate it.

The informal discussions will be needed because there will be many practical questions that require specific contextual answers. There is also likely to be some reticence on the part of various groups or individuals, consisting of worries, misunderstandings and existing 'baggage' that is usually easy to resolve in one-on-one conversation with experienced enterprise-architects. If these concerns are not tackled, or not tackled well, they can undermine an EA initiative to the point where it may erode away all usable value: hence addressing these issues with appropriate respect is a critical success factor for EA.

When done well, this process should lead to informed executives; awareness and buy-in on EA across all departments; and concrete business-issues addressed, delivering identifiable business value.

Populate the model

This is not actually a PEAF process as such, but a sub-process that is used extensively elsewhere in the *Operate* phase, particularly in the PEAF processes 'Modelling the Current State' and Strategic Planning'.

The main PEAF *Products* used, created or referenced within these activities are the model-content, via the Toolset and in accordance with the Metamodel.

The key *Actors* within this process are the Enterprise Architect, Provider, SME, Owner, Modeller and Checker.

The sub-process starts from a provided business-question and the related scope. The activities are often iterative, researching new information and discussing the results with the Owner and other stakeholders for this part of the overall enterprise-model.

The key steps for this sub-process can be summarised as follows.

Collect the Information: The Enterprise Architect and Modellers would be responsible for verifying the scope, and, with the help of the Provider, Owner and appropriate SMEs, for identifying and retrieving all the sources of information needed to support the required modelling.

Quality-Assure the Information: Enterprise Architect and Checker will be responsible for fact-checking and other quality-assurance required to validate the information used, and ensure that the information is valid, complete, consistent and correct.

Load the Information: The Enterprise Architect, Modellers and others as required will enter the information into the EA toolset, in accordance with the Metamodel, and create new views into the enterprise model as appropriate.

Integrate the Information: The Enterprise Architect works with the Modeller to link and/or merge any new or updated information into the EA Model. A decision will need to be taken as to whether the EA Model will become the 'database of record' for each item. If so, governance will need to be applied to ensure that people no longer use the previous source. If not, procedures or interfaces will need to be defined to ensure future synchronisation of the EA Model with any future changes in the original source.

Present the Information: The Enterprise Architect and Modeller will collate all of the resultant information into one or more views (colloquially described as 'models'). This set of information is then presented to the stakeholders for review and sign-off.

In some cases, particularly when modelling Current State in an IT context, it may be possible to automate part of the process by use of data-extracts. The EA toolset will need the appropriate 'import' functionality, and considerable care will be needed in pre-import and post-import quality-checks and data-cleansing. A six-step method for doing this, together with a set of checklists for data-cleansing, is described in some detail within the 'Modelling the Current State' section of the *Operate* processes document in the PEAF specification.

Modelling the current state

This PEAF process addresses how to populate and maintain that part of the content of the EA toolset that describes the enterprise at the present time – the so-called Current State or 'As-Is' Model.

Every organisation is on an evolving journey, constantly adapting and re-shaping itself to respond to external internal changes and needs. To start any journey of change, knowing the start-point is one of the most important things to know. In effect, the Current State Model documents this 'problem space': once the model is documented to a sufficient level, it usually becomes apparent not only what areas need attention but also what likely changes are needed to address them. The current model also allows people to understand how changes in the present will affect the enterprise today and tomorrow.

Note that *no attempt should be made to document the entirety of the Current State*, as if the enterprise were a single static entity. Given the rate of change in most organisations, such an approach would usually be futile, doomed to failure even before it starts. Instead, a more pragmatic piecemeal approach should be applied, using the overlapping scopes from individual change-projects to extend the 'hologram' of the enterprise model.

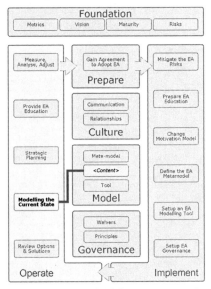

Products used in Modelling Current State

The main PEAF *Products* used, created or referenced within this process are the model-content, via the Toolset and in accordance with the Metamodel.

The key *Actors* within this process are Executive Management, Strategic Planning, Enterprise Architect, Provider, Modeller, SME, and Owner.

The process for populating the EA model is iterative, with each item of work building outward from a real 'business question' for which there is a real business need to be addressed. The first iteration is especially important because it starts from an empty model, and can affect the structure of everything that follows: the PEAF Metamodel can act as a valuable guide as to how to get started.

The key steps can be summarised as follows.

Determine the Question: Executive Management and the Strategic Planning team identify and describe the 'business question' that must be resolved. (At the more detailed layer, the same activity could also be carried out by programme-managers, project-team members and other architecture 'clients', defining an equivalent business-question for project-needs.) Typically the question either cannot be answered at present, or the confidence in any current answer is too low to be useful.

Determine the Scope: Enterprise Architect reviews the business-question and determines its scope in terms of the enterprise-architecture. (There is often a temptation to try to 'answer the question' straight away, but it is essential to resist this and focus on the explicit scope and information-needs instead.)

Populate the Model: The Enterprise Architect, Modellers and others source the required information, develop new or amended content in the EA Model, and create and present the required views, as described for the 'Populate the Model' sub-process.

Answer the Question: Working with the respective stakeholders, the Enterprise Architect uses the architecture-views to explore the various options and trade-offs posed by the context of the initial question.

Strategic planning

It is essential that enterprise-architects become active participants in the organisation's strategic planning.

Strategic planning may occur for many different reasons, such as introducing or divesting product-types, service-types or lines of business, cost-reduction or risk-reduction, or enhancing any other aspect of business agility, durability efficiency and effectiveness. Typical triggers include mergers and acquisitions, takeovers, and market or shareholder pressure. Whatever the reason, enterprise-architecture needs to be involved, to ensure alignment to overall aims of the organisation, and to ensure that impacts to Enterprise Debt are fully understood and addressed.

In essence, the Strategy Model identifies and describes the driving forces both behind the organisation as it currently stands, and the forces and reasoning behind the direction it will take towards its future.

This PEAF process provides a summary of enterprise-architecture activities that need to take place in its engagement with a typical strategic-planning exercise such as Annual Business Planning, that would create a portfolio of projects that will need to be executed during the next financial year.

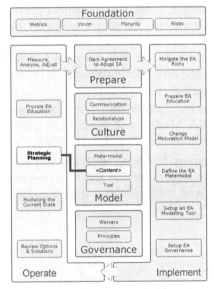

Products used in Strategic Planning

The main PEAF *Products* used, created or referenced within this process are the model-content, via the Toolset and in accordance with the Metamodel.

The key *Actors* in this process are Board of Directors, Executive Management, and Enterprise Architect.

This is described in two parts:

- *Create/Update Enterprise Strategy Model*
- *Create/Update Planning Models*

These represent guidelines only: the actual processes to be used in practice will need to be adapted to the organisation's needs and its existing processes for modelling and governance.

Create/Update Enterprise Strategy Model

The key steps for this part of the process can be summarised as follows.

Establish the Context: The Board of Directors will review and, if necessary, update the organisation's Vision, Mission, Goals and overall strategies. In parallel, Executive Management review and update the applicable Influences, whilst the Enterprise Architect performs risk-analysis such as via SWOT and similar techniques.

Establish Overall Strategy: Executive Management and Enterprise Architect review the current Tactics and Objectives in relation to the amended Strategies. The Executive also review Policies and Rules, whilst the Enterprise Architect would be responsible for reviewing any related performance-indicators, and for identifying and retrieving all sources of information needed to support these reviews.

Populate the Model: The Enterprise Architect, Modellers and others will develop new or amended content in the EA Model, and create the required views, as described for the 'Populate the Model' sub-process.

Present Enterprise Strategy Model: Enterprise Architect collates all of the resultant information into an Enterprise Strategy Model view. This is presented to the Board of Directors for review and sign-off.

Create/Update Planning Models

This part of the overall process may take place within the Strategy process, or else separately, such as in support of other approved projects, programmes or portfolios. All the steps in these activities are likely to incorporate the 'Populate the Model' sub-process as described earlier. The key steps for the set of planning-models can be summarised as follows.

Analyse Existing Models and Context: The Enterprise Architect and the Strategic Planning team review and re-assess the Strategy Model, the context and implications for Enterprise Debt, and the description of the enterprise current-state as represented by the content in the EA toolset.

Create Target Structural Model: The Enterprise Architect and Modellers create a Target Structural Model within the EA toolset, representing the overall context of the enterprise, in terms of the Metamodel, at the completion of the actions outlined within the Strategy Model. The required activities are much as described for the Strategy Model: collect information, quality-assure that information, load it into the EA toolset, and create integrated views as required.

Create/Update Intermediate Models: The Enterprise Architect and Modellers create similar views that represent the 'enterprise state' at various intermediate points in time, as required, between the present time and the implied end-point of the Strategy Model. Typically these will be at half-yearly or yearly intervals, or at other points linked to budgeting cycles, statutory reporting-cycles or similar events. These views should be extracted or derived from comparisons between the Current Model and Target Model, as perhaps amended or extended from the results of the information-gathering, validation and other activities summarised above.

Create/Update Portfolio Model: The Enterprise Architect, Strategic Planning team and the Change Management team collaborate to define and specify a portfolio of change-projects to implement the changes indicated in the Target Model and Intermediate Models. This is presented to the Executive Management for review, and forwarded to the Board of Directors for sign-off.

Review options and solutions

The purpose of governance is to ensure that as change happens on a daily basis, each change is guided in accordance with the larger strategic and long term picture of the enterprise. This is the point where enterprise-architecture meets solution-architecture: it is the governance processes that provide the key bridge between them.

Governance should not put up barriers to prevent work from happening, but should allow decisions to be made in the context of the implications and the Enterprise Debt that may be incurred.

Whilst strategic plans will be in place for the organisation, events can overtake an enterprise, such that those plans need adjustment. By the time work gets down to the projects and programmes to carry out the work, the strategic intent could become lost amongst the day-to-day detailed focus of projects. The role of governance is to identify any deviations from the recommended architectures, 'surfacing' the details of those deviations such that clear business decisions can be made. This ensures that everything keeps on track to the overall aims of the enterprise.

The main focus of governance is on *Why*, *What* and *How*, with an emphasis on:

- *Principles* – Over-arching statements that convey the philosophy, direction or belief of an organization; serve to guide people in making the right decisions for the organization.

- *Policies* – Focus on desired results, not on means of implementation; describes required actions, may include pointers to standards.

- *Standards* – Mandatory action or rule to support and conform to a policy; should make a policy more meaningful and effective.

EA governance comes into play before any projects are initiated, and as soon as the business encounters a problem or determines a requirement indicating changes to the enterprise (organisational structure, processes, locations, sales-channels, applications, etc). It continues a watching brief as projects develop, in parallel with governance for solution and technical architectures.

Most project-processes involve some form of governance and/or funding 'gateways', shifting authority from high-level to low-level, from enterprise-architecture through solution-architecture and process- and technical-architectures. The 'Review Options & Solutions' process described here is a generic summary of what needs to occur in practice, and should be tailored to align with the organisation's needs and existing project-management methods.

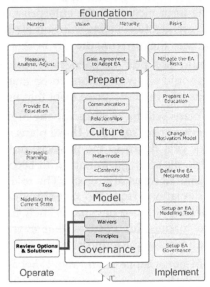

Products used in Review Options And Solutions

The main PEAF *Products* used or referenced in this process are Principles and Waivers.

The key *Actors* in this process are Strategic Investment Board, EA Review Board, and Solution Architect.

The key steps can be summarised as follows.

Review Problem: A Solution Architect creates a Business Problem Definition, and presents it to the EA Review Board for enterprise-architecture review. This ensures that the problem-definition is correctly framed, and does not include arbitrary assumptions about possible solutions to that business-problem. For example, a problem-statement of "the business-problem is that we need a CRM [Customer Relationship Management] system" would be rejected: instead, the problem-statement should describe the real underlying business needs.

Review Options: The Solution Architect creates a Solution Options document, with summaries of expected impact on Enterprise Debt for each option, and recommendations for proposed solutions. The EA Review Board assesses the implications to the enterprise-architecture and Enterprise Debt, to ensure that all options have been adequately considered and that the proposed solution is appropriate. The EA Review Board may also refer options to the Strategic Investment Board for further review, and discuss the implications with the Solution Architect, providing assistance to identify other solution-options that are more in alignment with architecture policy.

Review Solution: The Solution Architect creates a Solution Design document based on the option chosen from the previous step. The EA Review Board and Enterprise Architect work with the Solution Architect to amend and develop the respective solutions such as to reduce potential or existing Enterprise Debt. These assessments may be sent to the Strategic Investment Board for the final review and 'go/no-go' decision. The Solution Architect will then assist developers and others in creating and delivering the approved solution-design.

Measure, analyse and adjust

This process is concerned with utilising the metrics defined in the *Prepare* phase and gathering the associated data, analysing it to understand how effective the EA initiative is, and identifying and acting on the necessary ongoing adjustments to keep the EA effort on track.

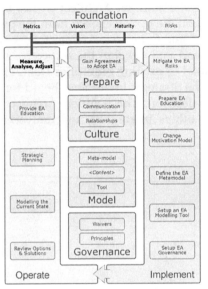

Products used in Measure, Analyse And Adjust

The main PEAF *Products* used or referenced in this process are Metrics, Vision and Maturity.

The key *Actors* in this process are Strategic Investment Board, EA Review Board, Executive Management, EA Project Board, and Enterprise Architect.

The key steps can be summarised as follows.

Measure: At regular intervals – typically monthly, and also at the end of the funded EA activity-period – the Enterprise Architect will gather the specified metrics, and also run polls and other methods to garner feedback on progress and utilisation of EA.

Analyse: The Enterprise Architect will analyse the results of the collected information, and produce recommendations for change in the EA processes, practices and governance. These will be passed to the Strategic Investment Board, EA Review Board, EA

Project Board and Executive Management for formal review and approval.

Adjust: The Enterprise Architect is responsible for ensuring that all of the approved changes are appropriately actioned.

Application

- Enterprise-architecture is ultimately the responsibility of *everyone* – not solely those with 'architect' in their job-title. How do you ensure that people throughout the enterprise not only acknowledge and understand that broader responsibility, but enact it in their day-to-day work? What materials and tactics do you need to apply in order to help them in this?

- What methods and model-types do you use in modelling the various aspects of the enterprise? For whom do you prepare each type of diagram, and why?

- How do you ensure that modelling is done in a pragmatic way, in accordance with real business needs? How do you prevent the common tactic – unfortunately encouraged by some EA frameworks – of attempting to 'boil the ocean' by modelling everything in the current-state, whether it is useful or not to do so? How do you ensure that each new item of modelling-work contributes towards the growth and clarity and usefulness of the overall enterprise model?

- In what ways do your enterprise-architecture processes link in with the broader strategic planning of the organisation? If your current EA scope is constrained to the IT domains, how can you ensure that what happens in IT does align appropriately to the broader organisational strategies – including concerns such as business-continuity and disaster-recovery, which will need information in some form even when the IT itself is out of action?

- What review-processes and governance-processes do you need in order to ensure that business changes and solution-options align appropriately with the overall goals of the organisation? What 'teeth' do you need to ensure that this does indeed happen? And how and via what means do you monitor 'success' in those terms?

- How do you monitor the value and success of enterprise-architecture itself? By what means and metrics can you prove its business-value to others? By what means and processes would you measure, analyse and adjust the functioning of the architecture itself, to ensure that it continues to grow in its maturity and capability on behalf of the overall organisation?

- And what support – if any – do your existing EA frameworks provide you, for any or all of this? What aspects of the everyday 'doing' of enterprise-architecture do they cover? What's missing? What do you need to change, in order for the enterprise-architecture to deliver greater value to the business of the business?

INTO PRACTICE

Summary

This final section provides some practical notes, guidance and 'lessons-learned' from implementing PEAF in a wide variety of different types of organisations.

Details

The importance of lessons-learned

There's a painful old joke that asks "How do we develop good judgement? "By experience", is the answer. But then how do we gain that experience? "By bad judgement..."

More to the point, we don't develop that experience just by bad judgement, but by *learning* from the results of that bad judgement. And the quickest and wisest way to get real value is to learn from other people's 'bad judgement', rather than repeating all of those mistakes for ourselves.

The whole aim of PEAF is to get people started in their enterprise-architecture, with an emphasis on doing the minimum number of things to get the maximum impact. All of PEAF is about getting 'into practice', as quickly as possible, yet avoiding all of the errors that so often cause problems for the EA, either straight away or further down the track.

In effect, every part of PEAF represents a 'lesson learned'. Every item in PEAF – whether Product or Process – is in the framework because the absence of that item, or absence of clarity around that item, has been seen to cause *practical* problems in the development of the architectures or in the enterprise-architecture capability.

For example, everyone knows that it's necessary to model things in the enterprise-architecture: processes, infrastructures, the inter-connections and inter-dependencies between anything and just about everything else. Yet time after time, much of the value is lost because of attempts to 'boil the ocean', modelling everything in sight rather than focussing on a single business-question at a time. The lesson here is that it's essential to identify that business-question *first*, then find the information-sources from which to

102

model it, do the model so as to answer the question, and move on the next. It does take a long time to build up a complete 'current state' model: but doing it the PEAF way will start to deliver real business value straight away, rather than spending vast amounts of time and money developing 'The Model' that probably never delivers any business value at all because it's already long out of date by the time it's complete. PEAF is all about being pragmatic, in a real business context.

Everything summarised in this book is included within PEAF because of someone's painful experience in the real-world practice of enterprise-architecture. It's there so that *you* don't have to go through the same pain. In short, if you want to avoid all manner of unneeded costs, in every sense, in setting up your enterprise-architecture, the real lesson-learned is to use PEAF.

A note on certification

Like many other enterprise-architecture frameworks, there's a set of certifications associated with PEAF. Unlike some of those other schemes, it seems, the reasons for certification in PEAF are purely pragmatic.

The purpose of certification in PEAF is twofold: to help people communicate with each other about architecture, and to ensure that people who are actively involved in enterprise-architecture do know how to avoid the many pitfalls for the inexperienced or the unwary.

It's for this reason that the only way to get PEAF certification is via an approved training-course. There is an exam at the end of each course, for each level of certification – and the pass-mark in each case is always 100%. This is because the only way in which the certification has any meaning is when the trainees *do* indeed understand everything they've been taught, and *do* know how to use it in real-world practice. The 100% pass-mark occurs in each case because if a participant doesn't get that pass-mark first time round, the trainer will continue to work with the student until they *do* reach the required level of practical understanding.

The point here is that certification, like everything else in PEAF, comes from another pragmatic lesson-learned: it must be *useful*, and it must deliver real business value, every time.

Application

- What are some of the practical lessons-learned that have arisen for you whilst reading this book? What would you now do differently in your enterprise-architecture as a result of reading this?

- How might you apply PEAF in your own organisation? Would you use it to help you get started in enterprise-architecture? Could you use it to help review the practices and processes of your existing EA capability? In what ways might you use PEAF to keep your architecture focussed on the real *pragmatic* needs of everyday business?

APPENDIX: SOURCES AND RESOURCES

Sources

The Pragmatic EA website is the official source for PEAF and all related materials. The full PEAF specification can be read online without charge on the site. It is also the reference-location for all the activities of the PEAF community.

- Pragmatic EA: see www.PragmaticEA.com

The concept of 'Enterprise Debt' is derived from the work of Ward Cunningham on 'Technical Debt' in software development:

- Technical Debt: see Wikipedia, en.wikipedia.org/wiki/Technical_debt

The following other frameworks and models were also referenced in the text:

- Zachman Framework: see Wikipedia, en.wikipedia.org/wiki/Zachman_Framework
- TOGAF (The Open Group Architecture Framework): see www.opengroup.org/togaf/
- FEAF ([US] Federal Enterprise ~Architecture Framework): see Wikipedia, en.wikipedia.org/wiki/Federal_Enterprise_Architecture
- Business Motivation Model: see www.omg.org/spec/BMM/
- ITIL (IT Infrastructure Library): see www.itil-officialsite.com

Other resources

Jeanne W. Ross, Peter Weill and David C. Robertson, *Enterprise Architecture As Strategy: creating a foundation for business execution* (Harvard Business School Press, 2006)

Tom Graves, *Doing Enterprise Architecture: process and practice in the real enterprise* (Tetradian, 2009)

Tom Graves, *Everyday Enterprise Architecture: sensemaking, strategy, structures and solutions* (Tetradian, 2010)

Lightning Source UK Ltd.
Milton Keynes UK
UKOW03f0032141013

218996UK00001B/1/P